Beautiful wire jewelry for beaders

Beautiful wire jewelry for beaders

Creative wirework projects for all levels

Irina Miech

Kalmbach Books

21027 Crossroads Circle
Waukesha, Wisconsin 53186
www.Kalmbach.com/Books

Published in 2009
13 12 11 10 09   3 4 5 6 7

Manufactured in the United States of America

Publisher's Cataloging-in-Publication Data

Miech, Irina.

   Beautiful wire jewelry for beaders : creative wirework projects for all levels / Irina Miech.

   p. : col. ill. ; cm.

ISBN: 978-0-87116-264-9

1. Jewelry making–Handbooks, manuals, etc. 2. Wire jewelry–Handbooks, manuals, etc. 3. Wire jewelry–Patterns. 4. Beadwork–Handbooks, manuals, etc. 5. Beadwork–Patterns. I. Title.

TT212 .M5434 2009

739.27

CONTENTS

INTRODUCTION

When I was a young girl, my father worked for the phone company and often brought home snippets of phone wire. Purple, red, yellow, green—this brightly hued wire captivated me. I taught myself how to make things from it; I created key chains, baskets, bowls, and little sculptures. I listened intently as my grandmother told stories of my great-grandfather, a jeweler, who had made custom designs out of gold wire.

As an adult, I traveled to Morocco, and it was there I learned to make my first earrings. This new direction was a breakthrough; with these skills, I could make more than just objects—I could make beautiful, wearable jewelry from wire. I have been experimenting and creating with wire ever since.

Wire is a versatile element. It can give you a simple and clean look, yet it also lends itself to creating the organic and natural designs that I love. Wire can form the backdrop for your work, enhancing and complementing the main design elements. Wire can frame a beautiful stone or a piece of art.

Wire also lends itself to working with other metal components such as head pins and chain. For example, if you want to incorporate beads into a design that uses chain, the easiest way to do it is with wire. Using wire is the cleanest and simplest way to make earrings. Wire is sculptural, allowing you to create three-dimensional designs. In fact, wire can be shaped in nearly any manner you choose.

For me, beads and wire are intrinsically related. I think of wirework as the canvas and of beads as the dabs of color and texture on the palette; they illuminate the wire jewelry piece. Beads may often provide the inspiration for the project, and your choice of beads will determine the character of a piece. You may choose to celebrate nature with semiprecious stones and pearls, go for an exotic look with ethnic beads, or display other artists' work by using their art beads in your designs.

Throughout my 15 years of teaching wirework, I have developed my artistic style and my techniques for working with wire that I share with you in this book. I hope you enjoy taking an artist's journey through the versatile and elegant world of wirework, and I wish you great success making beautiful wire jewelry!

Arina Miech

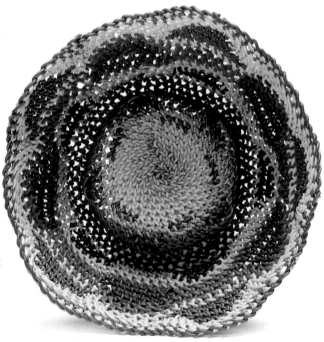

I wove these baskets out of telephone wire when I was about 8 or 9 years old. It was the beginning of a lifelong love of wirework.

HOW TO USE THIS BOOK

I designed the projects in this book as an introduction to wirework. As a beader, you probably have had plenty of experience stringing beads on flexible beading wire. Many beautiful beaded bracelets and necklaces can be made this way. But because you are reading this book, I know you are interested in expanding your set of jewelry-making skills. When you learn the basic wirework skills presented in these projects, you will be amazed at the doors that open for you. You can venture beyond bracelets and necklaces to shape your own pendants, earrings, rings, pins, clasps, and other jewelry components.

The skill level required for each project progresses gradually from beginner through intermediate to advanced. Each project builds upon the previous, and with each project you'll learn a new wireworking technique through detailed, step-by-step photos with written explanations. I've also included finishing instructions for each jewelry piece.

If this is your first experience working with wire, I suggest that you start with the first project, Uptown Chic, in which you'll learn how to make a plain loop—a key technique in many wire designs. The second project in the book, Burst of Color, introduces the technique for making a wrapped loop. Continue working your way through the projects without skipping any, and you'll build a solid foundation of wirework skills.

Those who have experience with wire, particularly those who have practiced and mastered the basic techniques that are reviewed on pages 15–18, should be able to choose a project that matches their experience level, follow the step-by-step instructions, and finish the project successfully.

I designed several options for each project to jump-start your creative thinking. If you like, elaborate on the theme, the techniques, or the look of the featured jewelry by combining and improvising, using what you've learned to create your own variations.

The wire needed for the projects is round wire unless specified in the materials list as a different shape, such as half-round or square. All of the wire, beads, and findings used in my projects came from Eclectica, the bead store I operate in Brookfield, Wisconsin. I encourage you to support your local bead and craft stores as you look for your project supplies. Enjoy making the project your own as you choose beads and other components!

Each project includes a few extra ideas that show how I took the technique in new directions. The gray backgrounds of these photos will help you distinguish these variations from the main project.

ABOUT WIRE

Wire is an essential material for many jewelry designs, and **sterling silver wire** is the foundation for all of the projects in this book.

If you're new to shaping wire, you may want to practice the basic techniques shown on pages 15–18 with copper or silver-coated copper wire. As you build confidence in your ability to manipulate wire, you can progress to using sterling silver wire.

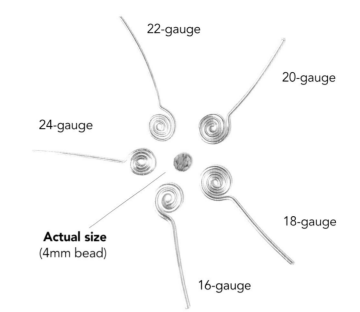

Actual size
(4mm bead)

Wire gauges

Wire comes in many different **gauges**, or thicknesses. The larger the number, the smaller the diameter of the wire. Most of the wire you'll use for projects in this book is either 22- or 24-gauge.

Occasionally a project will call for a heavier gauge, such as 18-gauge wire for the Whimsical Pins (page 48) and 16-gauge wire for the Leaf Silhouettes (page 97).

Keep in mind that the hole size of your beads will limit the diameter of wire that can be used with them; pearls typically have very small holes, for example, requiring a finer gauge wire.

This system of gauging wire is used primarily in the United States. Other countries gauge wire by its metric measurement (see the gauge equivalents chart to the right).

Wire shapes

Round wire is the most common wire shape. Because the majority of the projects in this book call for that shape, you can assume the wire needed is round unless otherwise specified. Other common shapes are half-round and square. These wire shapes can create certain effects such as the twisted free-form frame for a stone (page 87).

Wire temper

Temper refers to the hardness of the wire. Three tempers of wire are made: dead-soft, half-hard, and full-hard. They range from very pliable to very stiff.

The projects in this book call for either **dead-soft** or **half-hard** wire, as specified in the materials list. Dead-soft wire can be manipulated easily—even bent with your fingers. I use dead-soft when I need to do a lot of shaping or wrapping. Half-hard wire has more resistance and retains its shape better. If the shaping to be done is minimal and strength is important, use half-hard wire.

All wire hardens as you manipulate it; this is called **work-hardening**. Work-hardened pieces are stronger and they hold their shapes better than softer wire. To work-harden wire after it is shaped, place it on a bench block and tap the work very gently with a metal hammer. If you use force, the wire will flatten as it hardens. Tapping with a rawhide or nylon mallet is another way to work-harden the wire.

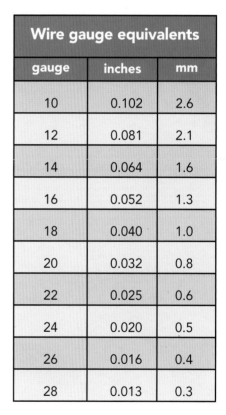

Wire gauge equivalents		
gauge	inches	mm
10	0.102	2.6
12	0.081	2.1
14	0.064	1.6
16	0.052	1.3
18	0.040	1.0
20	0.032	0.8
22	0.025	0.6
24	0.020	0.5
26	0.016	0.4
28	0.013	0.3

In the project instructions, most measurements are given in inches with a metric equivalent (rounded to the nearest whole number); bead sizes are given in metric, the worldwide standard for measuring beads.

WIREWORKING TOOLS AND SUPPLIES

roundnose pliers

chainnose pliers

flatnose pliers

To create beautiful wire jewelry, you need quality tools. Think of your tools as an extension of your hands. When you shop for your first set of wireworking tools, purchase pliers designed specifically for making jewelry, and buy the best quality you can afford. The better the quality of your pliers, the more enjoyable it will be to work with them.

Ergonomically designed tools have soft, comfortable grips that reduce stress on your hands. Often the handles are longer as well. Because I work with my tools every day, I prefer using an ergonomic design.

Everyone who begins working with wire acquires a set of basic tools in the beginning, and below I outline the **basic tool set** you'll need to complete the projects in this book. You'll also see exactly what's required for a specific project in the **tools and supplies** lists at the beginning of each project.

Roundnose pliers are used to make loops and rounded curves and to start spirals. The nose of these pliers is cone-shaped, which allows you to make loops of various sizes. Working at the tip gives you a very tight loop; working at the base makes wider loops or curves.

The nose of my pliers is $^{13}\!/_{16}$ in. (21mm) long. The point at which you form the loop on the cone-shaped nose determines the size of

the loop created. Experience and practice will help you find the point that produces the size of loops that you like. To make consistently sized loops, you can mark the pliers with permanent marker and always work at the same point.

Chainnose pliers have narrow, tapered jaws. They are used to bend and manipulate wire, and are especially useful for working in tight spaces. Two pairs can be used together for opening and closing jump rings, or use a pair of chainnose and a pair of flatnose pliers to do this.

Flatnose pliers, with wide, smooth jaws, are used to create broad bends in wire and for holding spiral components flat while shaping.

2nd step
7mm

3rd step
10mm

1st step
5mm

small stepped wire-wrapping pliers

Stepped wire-wrapping pliers are used much like roundnose pliers to create uniformly sized rings or loops. One jaw has three steps for shaping three different sizes. The clear plastic guard on the other jaw lets you work without marring the wire. The projects call for two sizes of these pliers: small and large (see photos below for sizes).

Tool Magic is very helpful for beginning wireworkers. Dip the jaws of any pliers in this liquid and let it dry into a rubbery coating to help prevent damage to wire.

Crimping pliers are used with crimp beads to attach clasps or other findings to flexible beading wire.

Nylon-jaw pliers are used to straighten wire. Hold one end of the wire with chainnose pliers and pull the wire slowly through the non-marring nylon jaws to smooth out any bends or kinks.

Side cutters are the most common type of cutter used to cut wire for jewelry making. The term "side cutters" describes any cutters with blades that are parallel to the handles. Within the side cutters category, you can choose the type of cutting blades you prefer. You'll find trade-offs between blade durability, cutting power, and the shapes left on the cut wire ends. **Bevel cutters** are durable, economical, and can cut very thick wire. They leave pronounced V shapes on the wire ends, so if your design requires flat ends, you'll need to file them. On the other end of the cutting spectrum are **super-flush cutters**, which leave flat wire ends. These cutters are best reserved for wire that's thinner than 18-gauge.

For me, a good choice in side cutters is **multipurpose flush cutters**, which fall between bevel cutters and super-flush cutters in durability and cut. I use my flush cutters to cut precious-metal wire as well as flexible beading wire. If you prefer to use super-flush cutters, which aren't designed for cutting beading wire, or you simply want to prolong the life of your primary cutters, purchase a second pair of inexpensive bevel cutters and use them for cutting only beading wire.

A caution: Although none of the projects in this book call for memory wire, keep in mind that you must use **memory wire cutters** to cut this material—never use the side cutters you use for precious-metal wire or you will damage them.

crimping pliers

nylon-jaw pliers

multipurpose flush cutters

2nd step 16mm
3rd step 20mm
1st step 13mm

large stepped wire-wrapping pliers

tool coating

11

pin vise

cup bur

bench block

A **pin vise** is a hand tool with a collet (or chuck) at one end. By tightening the collet around the end of a wire or wires, I can use it to twist square wire and to twist multiple wires together. The pin vise can also hold other bits such as drill bits, bead reamers, or cup burs.

A **cup bur** is used to round and smooth the ends of wire and is especially helpful when making earring wires. The cup holds tiny file teeth that smooth the wire end as you turn the tool clockwise (counterclockwise if you're left-handed).

A **bench block** is a polished steel surface used for flattening, straightening, or hardening wire. A 2-in. (51mm) square block is large enough for making most wire jewelry projects. Blocks may be solid steel or may be made of wood with a steel surface.

A **chasing hammer** has one large, very slightly convex face, used for flattening and hardening. The other end is ball shaped and is used for texturing. For wire jewelry projects such as the ones in this book, a hammer with about a 1-in. (26mm) face will work well.

A **sharpening stone** is used to file a wire end to a smooth point. You'll use this tool when you create pins, such as those on pages 48 and 78.

Files come in a variety of shapes and sizes. For the projects in this book, I recommend getting a **set of mini files** in a variety of profiles, including flat, round, and half-round.

Although you can use nearly any kind of cylinder as a mandrel, tools are made specifically for this purpose. A **stepped ring mandrel** is a cone-shaped tool that has steps marked with a range of ring sizes. For working with wire, use a steel ring mandrel.

stepped ring mandrel

sharpening stone

mini files

chasing hammer

A cone-shaped **bracelet mandrel** is used to measure and shape bracelets. For working with wire, I recommend an oval steel mandrel.

You'll need a **ruler** for every project in the book. I like a short, see-through ruler with both metric (the standard for measuring beads) and Imperial (inch) markings (commonly used in the United States).

Tweezers are handy for picking up small beads and for use with liver of sulfur solution.

Head pins are short lengths of wire with a stopper at the bottom to hold beads in place. Purchased head pins may have a simple stopper that looks like a nail head, or they may have a decorative detail. The most common gauges of head pins are 24- and 22-gauge. I usually use 24-gauge or finer for making wrapped loops and 22-gauge or thicker for making plain loops. A convenient

length is 2 in. (51mm), although in many projects, 1½ in. (38mm) will be long enough. Keep a supply of these on hand.

The most common **earring wire** style, and the easiest to make by hand, is the French hook. Other types, such as the secure lever-back style, can be purchased.

Jump rings are available in many diameters and wire gauges, both open (unsoldered) and soldered. Keep a supply handy; most of the projects call for open jump rings.

From the tiniest link to the largest, **chain** adds movement to jewelry designs. Chain can also be used to create a necklace extender; pair chain with a hook, and you have an adjustable necklace. Jewelry supply stores will cut chain off large spools, so you can usually buy just the length needed for a project.

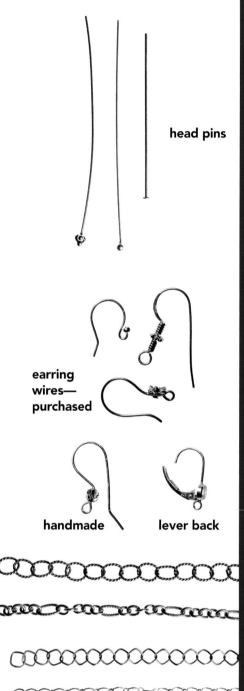

head pins

earring wires— purchased

handmade   lever back

chain styles

bracelet mandrel

open jump rings

soldered jump rings

tweezers

ruler

13

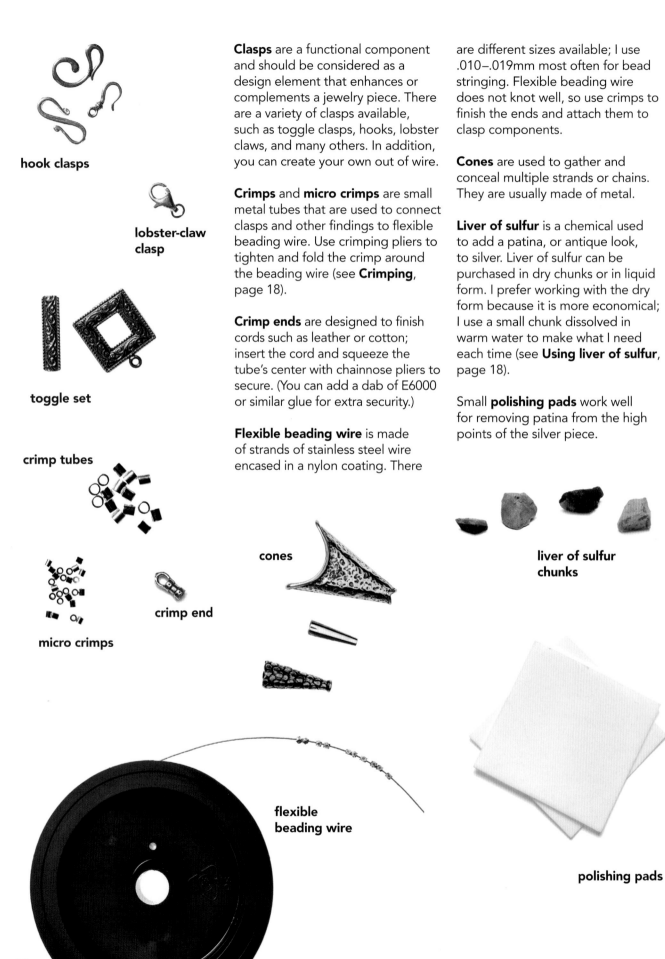

hook clasps

lobster-claw clasp

toggle set

crimp tubes

micro crimps

crimp end

cones

flexible beading wire

liver of sulfur chunks

polishing pads

Clasps are a functional component and should be considered as a design element that enhances or complements a jewelry piece. There are a variety of clasps available, such as toggle clasps, hooks, lobster claws, and many others. In addition, you can create your own out of wire.

Crimps and **micro crimps** are small metal tubes that are used to connect clasps and other findings to flexible beading wire. Use crimping pliers to tighten and fold the crimp around the beading wire (see **Crimping**, page 18).

Crimp ends are designed to finish cords such as leather or cotton; insert the cord and squeeze the tube's center with chainnose pliers to secure. (You can add a dab of E6000 or similar glue for extra security.)

Flexible beading wire is made of strands of stainless steel wire encased in a nylon coating. There are different sizes available; I use .010–.019mm most often for bead stringing. Flexible beading wire does not knot well, so use crimps to finish the ends and attach them to clasp components.

Cones are used to gather and conceal multiple strands or chains. They are usually made of metal.

Liver of sulfur is a chemical used to add a patina, or antique look, to silver. Liver of sulfur can be purchased in dry chunks or in liquid form. I prefer working with the dry form because it is more economical; I use a small chunk dissolved in warm water to make what I need each time (see **Using liver of sulfur**, page 18).

Small **polishing pads** work well for removing patina from the high points of the silver piece.

WIREWORKING TECHNIQUES

Working from the wire coil

Fundamental to my wireworking style is working from the wire coil. If you cut small lengths for each step, you'll need to trim the excess, thus accumulating a lot of short bits of wasted wire. Working from the coil is not only more economical, but it's also a real time-saver because it eliminates several cutting and trimming steps each time.

One important step to keep in mind: If you are making plain or wrapped loops, place the bead on the wire first! If you forget and make one loop before you string the bead, you can string the bead on the other wire end—but it's easier if you remember to do it first.

I begin with no more than 10 feet (3m) of coiled wire. Heavier-gauge wire is often sold in shorter coils; for example, my 18-gauge wire starts out as a 5-foot (1.5m) coil. As you work, just keep using the wire until it is too short to complete a component.

Unless the project instructions specify a cut length for a step, assume you are working from the wire coil. I hope you'll find, as I have, that this is a much more efficient way to work, and it will streamline your wireworking projects.

Some instructions call for forming loops over beads on head pins. The process for making basic loops and

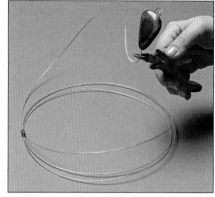

Working from the wire coil is more efficient than cutting short lengths of wire for each step.

wrapped loops is very similar whether you are using a head pin or working from the wire coil.

Making a basic loop above a bead

1 String a bead on a head pin or the wire coil. With your fingers, make a right-angle bend over the bead.

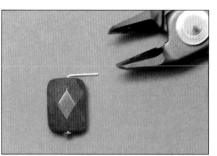

2 With side cutters, trim the wire to ⅜ in. (9.5mm).

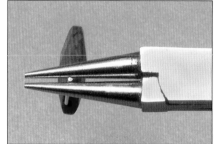

3 Grasp the wire end with the roundnose pliers.

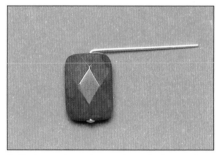

4 Roll the wire in the opposite direction of the bend in a continuous motion until it forms a full circle.

5 Adjust the position of the pliers in the loop to continue rolling, if necessary. You may attach another component before closing the loop completely.

6 Use chainnose pliers to close the loop completely.

To make loops on both sides of the bead, work from the coil and repeat the process on the opposite side.

Making a wrapped loop and tucking the wire end

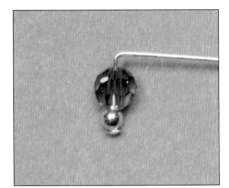

Begin a wrapped loop:
1 String a bead on a head pin or the wire coil. Grasp the wire with the tip of the chainnose pliers (just above the bead if on a head pin, and 1¼ in./ 32mm from the end if on the wire coil). Use your fingers to bend the wire over the pliers at a 90° angle.

2 Place the roundnose pliers in the bend of the wire as shown.

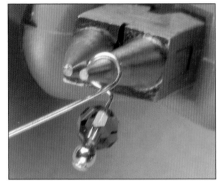

3 Wrap the wire over the top jaw of the roundnose pliers until it touches the bottom jaw. Loosen your grip, rotate the pliers 90° counterclockwise (if you are left-handed, rotate clockwise), and continue wrapping the loop around the bottom jaw of the pliers.

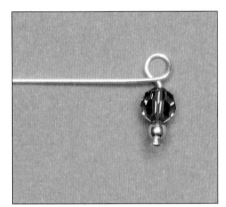

4 If necessary, center the loop over the bead by turning the pliers slightly counterclockwise while holding the bead. (If you are left-handed, rotate clockwise.) When the loop is centered, the wires should cross at a 90° angle. You may attach a component to the loop at this point.

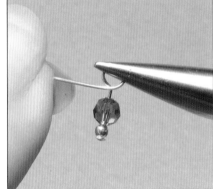

Finish the loop:
5 Holding the loop with chainnose pliers, use your fingers or a second set of pliers to grasp the wire end.

6 Wrap the wire into the gap between the loop and the bead, starting next to the loop. Make 2–3 wraps.

7 Trim the wire end close to the wraps.

8 Use chainnose pliers to tuck the wire end tightly between the wraps and the bead.

I am right-handed, and the photos show the actions as I do them. Most left-handers will need to use a mirror-image motion.

Making spirals

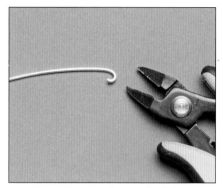

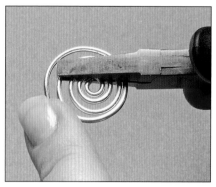

1 Make a loop at the end of the wire with roundnose pliers; trim the tip of the loop if it is not curved.

2 Continue shaping the wire to form a second loop around the first.

3 Grasp the spiral with flatnose pliers and turn the spiral while guiding the wire with your finger. Loosen the grip, regrip the spiral, and continue shaping until the spiral is the desired size.

Hammering

Use the smooth, slightly convex face of the chasing hammer to flatten and harden your wirework. Use the rounded end to add texture.

Work on a bench block placed on a solid, sturdy work surface. For the best control of your hammer, grasp it at its base.

Pay careful attention so you can control the points on the wire that become flattened or textured.

To flatten wire: With careful aim, you can control how wide the wire gets and at which points it spreads.

To add texture: The rounded end will add small divots of texture to the wire. Tap the piece while moving around the surface of the wire.

Smoothing wire ends

This technique is especially handy for finishing earring wires so they are smooth and comfortable to wear.

Place the wire end in the cup bur and turn the tool in short rotations clockwise (counterclockwise if you're left-handed).

Check with your fingertip to feel if the end of the wire is smooth. Repeat if necessary.

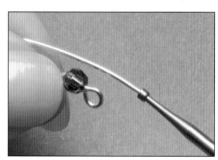

Rotate the cup bur in one direction only rather than using a back-and-forth motion. This will optimize the life of the tool.

Crimping

If your project is strung on flexible beading wire, a secure way to finish it is using a crimp tube (often referred to simply as a crimp). This is the most common way to attach clasps such as toggle clasps and hooks.

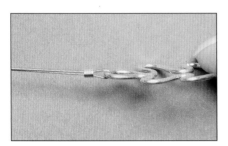

1 On flexible beading wire, string a crimp tube and a component (usually half of the clasp). String the wire back through the crimp.

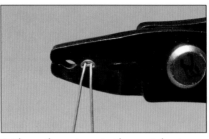

2 Place the crimp in the notch at the back of the crimping pliers, making sure the wires are separated. Squeeze to tighten.

3 Move the crimp into the notch near the tip of the pliers. Place the wires vertically in the notch, and squeeze to fold the crimp. Tug the wires to be sure they are secure.

Making Z-bends

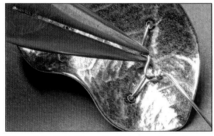

To add detail and tighten tension on a wire: Grasp the wire with flatnose pliers and rotate to form a small Z shape.

Using stepped wire-wrapping pliers

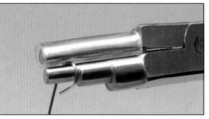

The three steps on these pliers help you make large, consistently sized curves, rings, or loops. Try wrapping wire at each step to see the results.

Opening jump rings and basic loops

To open: Using two sets of pliers, grasp one end of the ring in the tip of each pliers. Move one set of pliers toward you and one away to open the ring slightly. **To close:** Reverse the motion. Use the same method to open a basic loop, add components, and close the loop.

Using liver of sulfur

Dip silver in liver-of-sulfur solution to add a beautiful sheen, or patina, in a progression of colors starting with amber and ranging through magenta, blue, dark gray, and black.

Use liver of sulfur with proper ventilation; avoid breathing the fumes and avoid skin contact. Work near running water or keep a container of cool water handy to stop the action of the solution. After drying the piece, use a small polishing pad to highlight the raised areas, leaving the patina in the recesses for an antique look.

To use: In a small plastic container dedicated to use with liver of sulfur, dissolve a chunk in about a cup of warm water. The water will turn light yellow, and you will smell the strong odor of sulfur (like rotten eggs).

Immerse your silver piece (it's fine to drop it in the solution). When you see a patina color you like, remove the piece with tweezers, rinse in cool water, and dry. Repeat the process to darken the patina if desired.

necklace and earrings

Uptown Chic

This project is your introduction to forming a basic loop—the building block of wirework. After you master the loop, you will be amazed at the variety of designs you can create with this simple technique.

TO MAKE THE NECKLACE

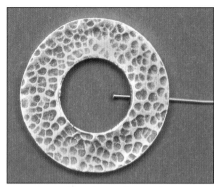

1 String a head pin through one side of the donut.

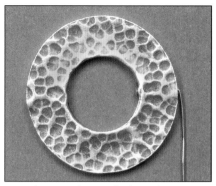

2 Make a right-angle bend over the donut.

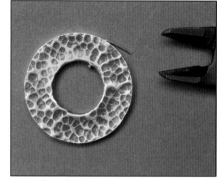

3 With side cutters, trim the head pin to ⅜ in. (10mm).

You'll need

Materials

24–30 in. (61–76cm) 22-gauge, half-hard wire
1¼ in. (32mm) donut
Assorted faceted gemstone beads, 4–10mm
Toggle clasp
5 13mm oval components
23mm oval two-hole component
6 in. (15cm) medium-link chain
12 barbell beads (see page 22)
27mm tube bead
2 earring wires
2 1½-in. (38mm), 22-gauge head pins

Tools and supplies

Chainnose pliers
Roundnose pliers
Side cutters
Ruler

 For another look at making basic loops, see page 15.

4 Grasp the wire end with the roundnose pliers about ¼ in. (7mm) from the tip of the pliers.

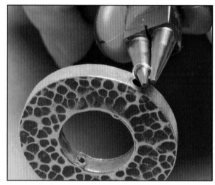

5 Roll the wire in the opposite direction of the bend in a continuous motion until it forms a full circle.

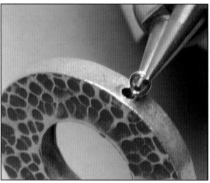

6 Adjust the position of the pliers in the loop to continue rolling, if necessary.

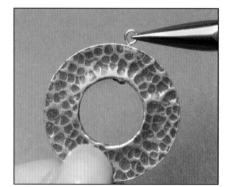

7 If needed, use chainnose pliers to adjust the loop so that the beginning and the end of the loop meet.

 As you practice making basic loops, you'll find the point on the roundnose pliers that works to create the size loop you like—you may prefer loops that are larger or smaller than my basic loop size.

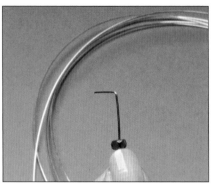

8 String a bead onto the wire coil and use chainnose pliers to bend the wire in a right angle ⅜ in. (10mm) from the end.

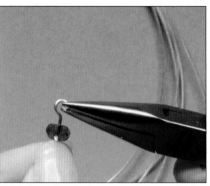

9 Make a basic loop at the end of the wire.

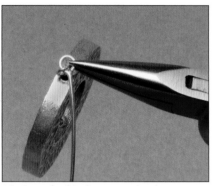

10 Attach this loop to the loop on the donut component: With chainnose pliers, open the loop slightly to the side, slide the other loop into it, and close it.

11 Slide the bead up the wire to the loop and make a loop on the other side of the bead. Continue adding basic-loop links on both sides of the donut in this way. Follow the design on page 20 or improvise to create your own.

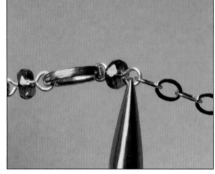

12 Cut the chain in half. On each necklace end, slide an end link of chain into a loop. Close the loop with chainnose pliers.

13 Working from the wire coil, slide a bead onto the wire, make a loop, and attach it to one end of the chain. Make a loop on the other side of the bead. Slide the ring of the clasp into the loop, and close the loop with chainnose pliers. Repeat for the other half of the clasp.

BARBELL BEADS: A CLOSER LOOK

This bead unit is made of 12 Hill Tribes silver beads strung on wire with a basic loop at each end. The barbell-shaped beads stack neatly in an X pattern, creating a lively component.

TO MAKE THE EARRINGS

String a bead onto the wire coil. Make a loop. Slide an oval component into the loop and close the loop. Make a loop on the other side of the bead. Slide an ear wire into the loop and close the loop. Repeat for the other earring.

Once you master making uniform basic loops, try linking them to silver rings, small donuts, or chain.

This set uses the same technique, but the colorful lampworked beads create a totally different look—fresh and playful.

Burst of Color

This project introduces the wrapped loop. Wrapped loops are more secure than basic loops, and they enable you to design with finer wire, which is important when working with beads with smaller holes.

You'll need

Materials

70–80 1½-in. (38mm), 24-gauge head pins
2 in. (51mm) extender chain
Lobster claw clasp
2 earring wires
70–80 2mm silver rounds
2 6 x 8mm crystal rondelles
85–95 4mm round crystals
16 ¾-in. (19mm) curved silver tubes
Flexible beading wire
2 crimp beads

Tools and supplies

Chainnose pliers
Roundnose pliers
Side cutters
Flexible beading wire cutters
Crimping pliers
Ruler

When making large quantities of wrapped-loop components, it's efficient to do them assembly-style: First, string beads on all head pins; second, make all of the loops; finally, wrap the loops and tuck the wire ends.

TO MAKE THE EARRINGS

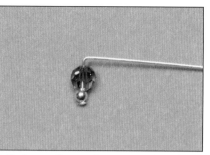

1 String a 2mm silver round and a 4mm crystal onto a head pin. Using the tip of the chainnose pliers to hold the head pin just above the crystal, make a right-angle bend over the pliers' jaw.

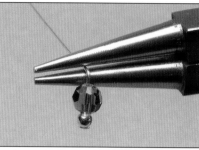

2 Place the roundnose pliers in the bend of the wire as shown.

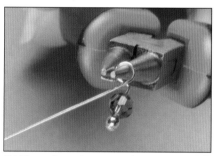

3 Wrap the wire over the top jaw of the roundnose pliers until it touches the bottom jaw. Loosen your grip, rotate the pliers 90° counter-clockwise (left-handers, rotate clockwise), and continue wrapping the loop around the bottom jaw of the roundnose pliers.

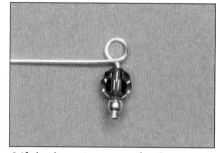

4 If the loop is not perfectly centered over the bead, bend the loop by turning the pliers slightly counter-clockwise while holding the bead. (If you are left-handed, rotate clockwise.) When the loop is centered, the wires should cross at a 90° angle.

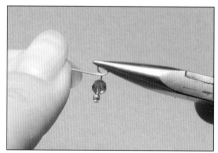

5 Holding the loop with chainnose pliers, grasp the wire end with your fingers or a second set of pliers.

6 Wrap the wire into the gap, starting next to the loop and moving toward the crystal. It should take 2–3 wraps to fill the gap.

7 Trim the end of the head pin close to the wraps.

8 Use chainnose pliers to tuck the wire end between the wraps and the bead.

9 Repeat steps 1–8 to make three components for each earring (six total). To finish the earrings, open the loop on an ear wire, string three components, and close the loop. Repeat for the other ear wire.

TO MAKE THE NECKLACE

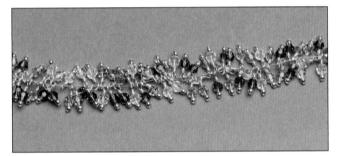

1 Make 60–70 wrapped-loop components as in steps 1–8 of the earrings directions. String the components on the flexible beading wire.

2 Group the wrapped-loop components as tightly together as possible. String a 6 x 8mm rondelle crystal and a curved tube on each side of the wrapped-loop components. Alternate crystals with tubes until you reach the desired length. Use crimps to attach the clasp to one end and the extender chain to the other.

3 Follow steps 1–4 of the earrings directions to begin three additional wrapped-loop components. Before wrapping the loops, string the components onto the last link of the extender chain.

4 Finish the wrapped loops to create dangles at the end of the extender chain.

I often create a decorative dangle for the end of an extender chain. This serves a practical purpose—to add a bit of weight to the end while giving the wearer something to grasp as she closes the necklace. The dangle can also mirror a design element—in this case, the dangles on the extender match the earring dangles.

With wrapped loops, you can build sturdy, secure bracelets and necklaces from almost any type of bead.

Focal bead by Anne Choi

A burst of wrapped-loop dangles creates a focal point above this toggle closure.

These wrapped loops connect to chain links and rings.

27

Crystal Rings

Chain adds movement and texture to your jewelry. Consider using chain as a connector between other components. In this project, the chain connects rings for an elegant look.

1 Working from the coil, begin a wrapped loop. Cut six ⅞–1-in. (22–26mm) pieces of chain, making them identical in length with an odd number of links. Wrap one length around a crystal ring and slide both ends onto the loop.

2 Finish wrapping the loop. String a bead onto the wire and slide it to the wrapped loop.

3 Begin a wrapped loop on the other side of the bead and use it to connect the ends of the chain length around another crystal ring. Finish the wrapped loop.

4 Repeat steps 1 and 2 to continue adding crystal rings, chain, and bead components until you reach the desired length. Connect half of the clasp to each end of the bracelet with a wrapped-loop bead component.

You'll need

Materials
15–20 in. (38–51cm) 22-gauge, half-hard wire
5–7 in. (13–18cm) small-link chain
3 20mm crystal rings
6–8 4mm round crystals

Tools and supplies
Chainnose pliers
Roundnose pliers
Flatnose pliers
Side cutters
Ruler

Create a fabulous pendant in a flash with a stone donut and chain.

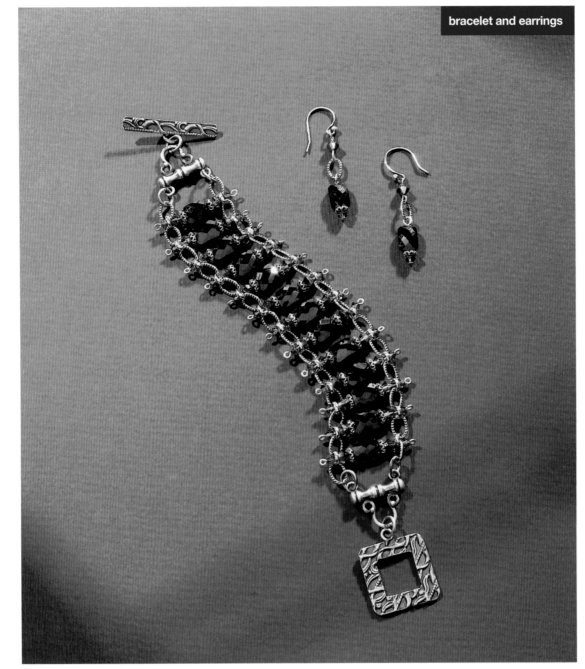

bracelet and earrings

Sparkling Ladder

This project is an exercise in making small, consistent loops. The bracelet design uses chain in an unconventional manner as its base.

You'll need

Materials

24–30 in. (61–76cm) 24-gauge, half-hard wire

8–12 in. (20–31cm) large-and-small-link chain
   (reserve 2 large links for the earrings)

2 1½-in. (38mm), 22-gauge head pins

2 earring wires

2 2-to-1 components

6 open jump rings

Toggle clasp

28–38 3mm bicone crystals

28–38 4mm bicone crystals

28–38 4mm spacers

15–20 8mm CZ rectangle beads

Tools and supplies

Chainnose pliers

Roundnose pliers

Flatnose pliers

Side cutters

Ruler

TO MAKE THE BRACELET

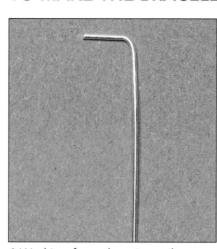

1 Working from the wire coil, use pliers to make a right-angle bend ³⁄₁₆ in. (5mm) from the wire end.

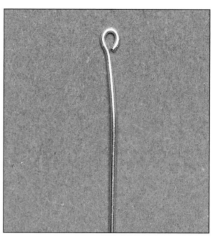

2 Working at the very tip of the roundnose pliers, make a tiny loop at the end of the wire to act as a stopper.

 As you consider the shape of the beads to use in this bracelet, keep in mind that flat beads work best.

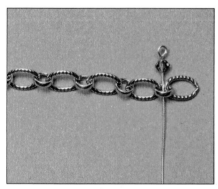

3 String a 3mm bicone crystal onto the wire, and then string the wire through the smaller of the links at one end of the chain.

4 String a 4mm crystal, a spacer, a CZ rectangle, a spacer, and a 4mm crystal.

5 String the wire through the small end link in the second length of chain. String a 3mm crystal.

6 Trim the wire to ³⁄₁₆ in. (5mm) below the crystal and make another stopper loop.

7 Continue adding rungs in this way until you reach the desired ladder length.

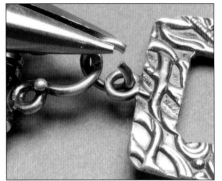

8 Open a jump ring and string one hole of the 2-to-1 component and the last link of one chain.

9 Close the jump ring. Repeat step 8 to connect the opposite chain to the remaining hole of the 2-to-1 component. Connect the second 2-to-1 component to the other side of the ladder in the same way.

10 Open a jump ring and string a 2-to-1 component and half of the clasp on each end.

The earrings are a playful take on the technique; start with just one bead on each rung and increase, then decrease, the bead count.

TO MAKE THE EARRINGS

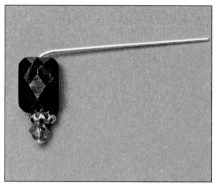

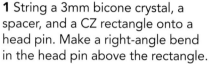

1 String a 3mm bicone crystal, a spacer, and a CZ rectangle onto a head pin. Make a right-angle bend in the head pin above the rectangle.

2 Trim the wire to ⅜ in. (10mm).

3 Make a loop using roundnose pliers.

4 Using chainnose pliers, slightly open the loop, slide on the reserved large link, and close the loop.

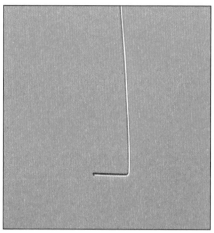

5 Working from the wire coil, use chainnose pliers to make a right-angle bend ⅜ in. (10mm) from the end of the wire.

6 Make a loop at the end and connect it to the chain link.

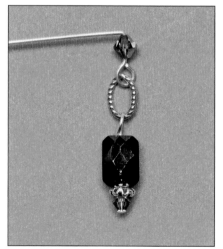

7 String a 4mm bicone crystal and make a right-angle bend above the bead.

8 Trim the wire to ⅜ in. (10mm).

9 Make another loop on the other side of the crystal. Before closing the loop, attach the ear wire.

Cornucopia of Gems

Cones are a pleasing design element with a practical purpose—they allow you to gather multiple strands and conceal wire ends.

You'll need

Materials

18–20 in. (46–51cm) 22-gauge, half-hard wire

20–24 in. (51–61cm) large-link chain

16–18 1½-in. (38mm) or 2-in. (51mm)
   24-gauge head pins

2 earring wires

Bail

2 small cones

Large cone

Assorted gemstone beads and crystals,
   3–10mm

Tools and supplies

Chainnose pliers

Roundnose pliers

Flatnose pliers

Side cutters

Ruler

 When selecting a cone, be sure it is wide enough to accommodate all of the elements you are planning to use and is long enough to conceal the ends of the chain, wire, or any other element that you don't want to show.

TO MAKE THE PENDANT

1 String a gemstone bead onto a head pin. Begin a wrapped loop. Before wrapping the wire, attach the component to a length of chain. Finish wrapping and tuck the wire end.

2 Make 10–12 chain components in various lengths using different groupings of gemstone beads and crystals. To make longer chain components, connect two shorter lengths of chain with a wire-wrapped gemstone link.

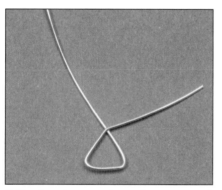

3 Begin a large, triangular wrapped loop.

4 Gather the ends of the chain components into the loop.

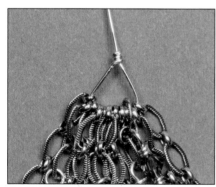

5 Finish wrapping the loop.

6 String the large cone over the grouping of chain components.

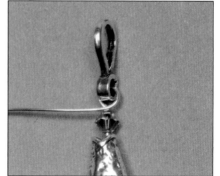

7 String a 4mm crystal on top of the cone. Begin a wrapped loop, string the bail, and finish the loop.

TO MAKE THE EARRINGS

Create coordinating earrings in the same way you created the pendant. Make two sets of three chain components and secure them within the small cones. Finish with a 3mm crystal over the cone, and attach to the earring wire with wrapped loops.

A large, petal-shaped cap makes a stylish substitute for a cone.

Using cones is an elegant way to gather multiple strands of beads strung on flexible beading wire.

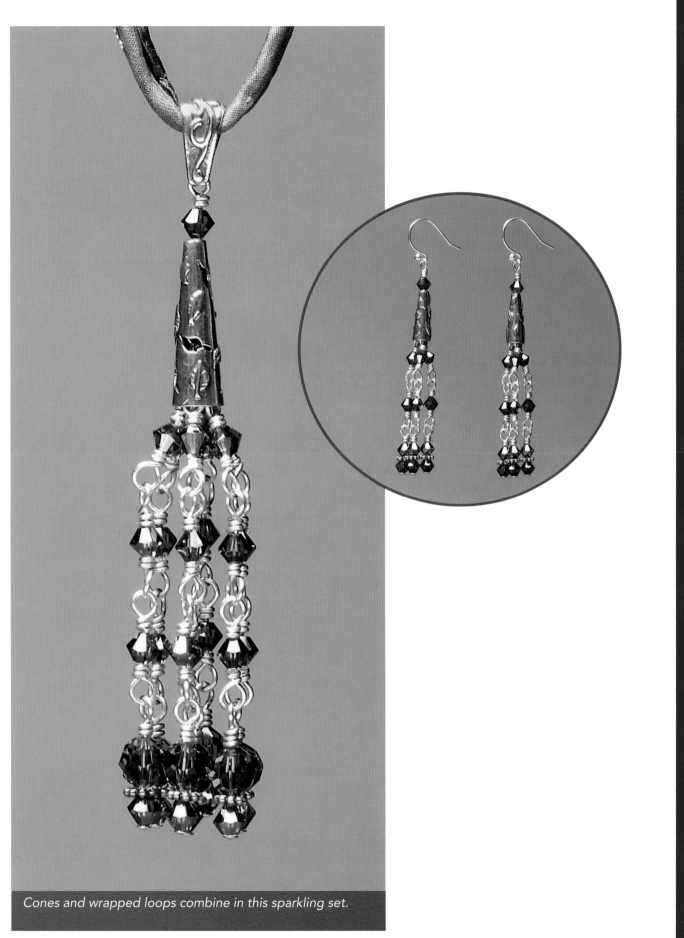

Cones and wrapped loops combine in this sparkling set.

necklace

On the Vine

Multihole pendants can be as versatile as a blank canvas.
In this project, you'll work with wire in a spontaneous and
free-form manner, creating a truly one-of-a-kind piece.

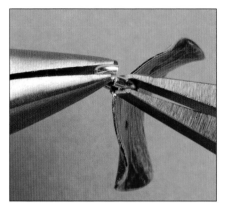

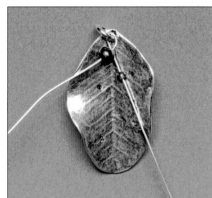

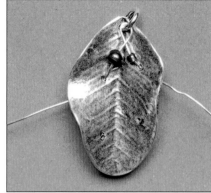

1 Attach a jump ring to the top hole of the leaf. Cut two 8–10-in. (20–25cm) lengths of wire.

2 Center the pendant on one wire. Cross the ends of the wire and string a bead on each end.

3 String each end from front to back through the nearest hole.

You'll need

Materials

24–30 in. (61–76cm) 24-gauge, dead-soft wire
2 crimp ends
2 in. (51mm) extender chain
Hook
4 open jump rings
24-gauge head pin
Bail
16–18 in. (41–46cm) leather cord
Assorted 3–8mm crystals and pearls
Multihole leaf component

Tools and supplies

Chainnose pliers
Flatnose pliers
Roundnose pliers
Side cutters
Ruler

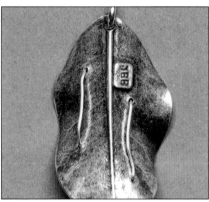

4 Turn the leaf over and string the two wire ends through the bottom holes from back to front.

5 On the front, twist the wire ends together. Trim one end, leaving the other long.

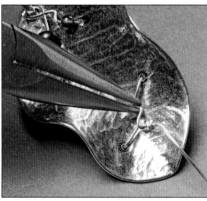

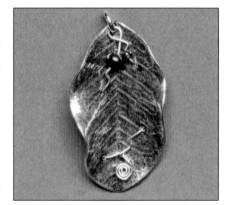

6 Tighten the wires by grasping and twisting with chainnose pliers to make soft zigzags.

7 Make a small spiral at the wire end.

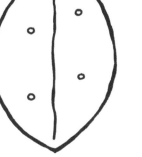

You can create your own multihole component by using a metal punch or a drill to make holes in a thin piece of any soft metal, such as silver or copper. Use this pattern for a leaf shape or design your own!

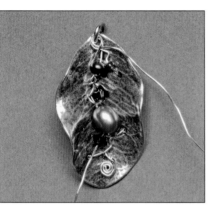

8 Center the pendant on a second wire and cross the ends. Add beads while weaving the ends in and out of the structure created by the first wire.

9 Fill gaps and embellish the pendant as desired. Occasionally wrap the wire around individual beads to create vine shapes.

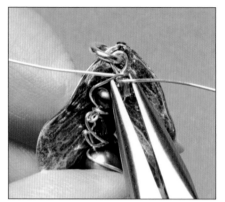

10 (If you feel your pendant is sufficiently embellished, skip this step.) Wrap a third 8–10-in. (20–25cm) piece of wire onto any other wire, centering it, and continue embellishing.

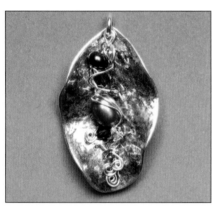

11 End each wire with a spiral.

12 Use a jump ring to connect the pendant to the bail.

13 String the leather cord through the bail.

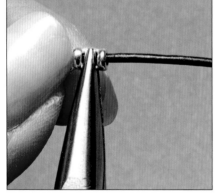

14 Use chainnose pliers to attach crimp ends to each end of the leather cord.

15 Use jump rings to connect the hook on one side and the extender chain on the other side. String a pearl on a head pin and attach it to the end of the extender chain with a wrapped loop.

FORMING SMALL SPIRALS

This technique is similar to forming a larger spiral as shown on page 17. Begin with a tiny bend made with chainnose pliers and don't trim the wire end.

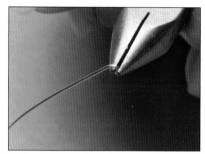

1 Make a tight bend working at the tip of the chainnose pliers.

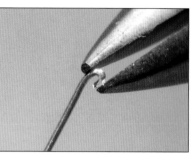

2 Tighten the bend with the tip of the pliers.

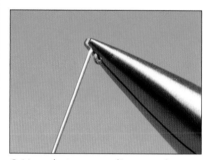

3 Use chainnose pliers to shape the beginning of the spiral: Grip, shape the wire with your fingers while turning the spiral, reposition the grip, and repeat.

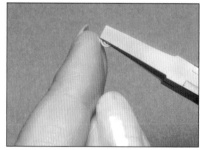

4 Switch to flatnose pliers and continue shaping.

5 Continue until the spiral is the desired size.

Use the holes in gemstone or shell beads as anchors for bead-embellished wire.

Here's the same leaf component in copper. Beaded wrapped-loop links made of copper wire alternate with copper rings.

Make your own leaf from metal clay and embellish it.

pendant and earrings

Hammered Spirals

The spiral is used in many cultures to signify life's journey. This timeless symbol can energize your jewelry designs!

You'll need

Materials

12 in. (31cm) 18-gauge, dead-soft wire

6–8 in. (15–20cm) 24-gauge, half-hard wire

2 earring wires

Bail

3 3mm silver rounds

3 cones

2 26mm gemstone drops

29mm gemstone drop

Flexible beading wire, .010mm

3 micro crimps

Tools and supplies

Chainnose pliers

Roundnose pliers

Flatnose pliers

Side cutters

Flexible beading wire cutters

Bench block

Chasing hammer

Ruler

Liver of sulfur (optional)

TO MAKE THE PENDANT

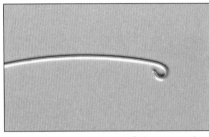

1 Working at the tip of the round-nose pliers, make a small loop.

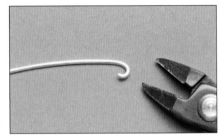

2 Cut off the very end of the loop if it is straight instead of curved.

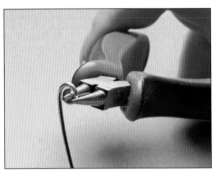

3 Continue looping the wire around the pliers to form a second loop around the first.

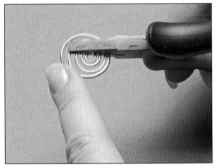

4 Using the flatnose pliers to grasp the spiral, shape the wire with your finger while you make a small clockwise turn with the flatnose pliers. Reposition the spiral in the pliers and continue shaping until the spiral is the desired size.

5 Place the spiral on the bench block. Holding the straight section of the wire, strike the spiral with the flat face of the hammer to flatten.

6 Switch to the rounded end and strike repeatedly across the spiral to create texture. Do not strike the straight section.

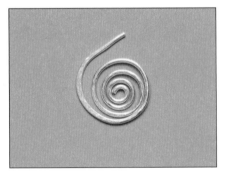

7 Cut the straight section of wire to ½ in. (13mm).

8 Make a loop at the end with the roundnose pliers.

9 Connect the loop to the bail. Use liver of sulfur to add patina if desired.

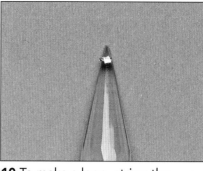

10 To make a loop, string the gemstone drop on beading wire. String both ends of the wire through a micro crimp, flatten the crimp with chainnose pliers, and trim the excess wire.

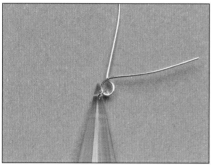

11 Using 24-gauge wire, begin a wrapped loop and string the beading-wire loop.

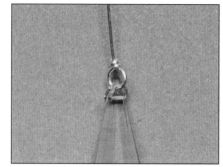

12 Finish wrapping the loop.

13 String the cone and a 3mm round bead on the wire.

14 Begin a wrapped loop.

15 Attach the drop to the spiral and finish the wrapped loop.

If your gemstone drops have holes that are large enough to accommodate 24-gauge wire, you can string the 24-gauge wire through the hole on the drop and forgo using the flexible beading wire and crimps shown in step 10.

TO MAKE THE EARRINGS

Create the earrings in the same
way you made the pendant but
slightly smaller. Attach ear wires to
the loops on the spirals and add
patina if desired.

*Use a hole punch designed for soft metal to make
holes in coins. Instant components!*

The spirals become links in this set.

Whimsical Pins

These pins are quick, fun projects, and the variations are endless.
This a great way to showcase a favorite bead.

You'll need

Materials

Basic Whimsical Pin
8–10 in. (20–25cm) 18-gauge, half-hard wire
Focal bead

Zigzag Whimsical Pin
10–14 in. (25–36cm) 18-gauge, half-hard wire
Focal bead
Assorted beads and spacers

Bead-Embellished Whimsical Pin
10–12 in. (25–31cm) 18-gauge half-hard wire
3 in. (76mm) 24-gauge, dead-soft wire
Focal bead
Assorted beads and spacers

Tools and supplies
Chainnose pliers
Roundnose pliers
Flatnose pliers
Side cutters
Bench block
Chasing hammer
Sharpening stone
Ruler

 When selecting focal beads for this project, look for large, flat stone or glass beads.

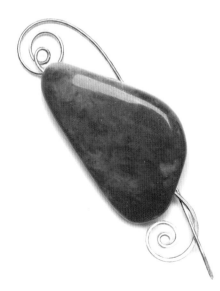

BASIC WHIMSICAL PIN

1 String a bead onto the 18-gauge wire. With roundnose pliers, start making a spiral.

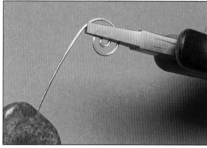

2 With flatnose pliers, continue shaping the spiral.

3 Hammer the spiral to flatten it slightly.

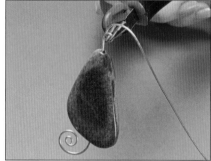

4 Move the bead above the spiral. Above the bead, use roundnose pliers to make a loop facing the opposite direction of the lower spiral.

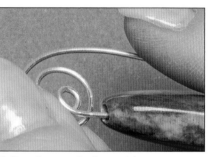

5 Continue spiraling with your fingers, coaxing the wire toward the back of the bead. Bring a length of straight wire behind the bead.

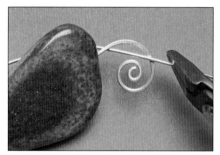

6 Pin the wire on the lower spiral hook. Trim the excess about ¼ in. (7mm) past the spiral hook.

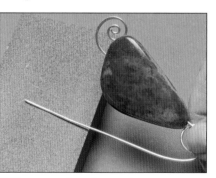

7 Sharpen the pin on the sharpening stone.

8 Lightly hammer the pin to work-harden it.

BEAD-EMBELLISHED WHIMSICAL PIN

Plan the look of the finished bead by dividing your beads into three sets. For the first set, strung on the main wire, I used a crystal, a silver spacer, and a focal bead.

For embellishment over the focal bead, I used freshwater pearls and silver spacers—these are the second set, strung on the 24-gauge accent wire. I finished with more silver beads and a crystal on the main wire.

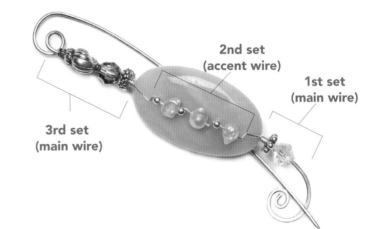

2nd set (accent wire)

1st set (main wire)

3rd set (main wire)

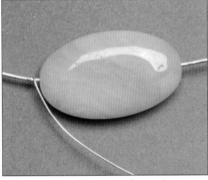

1 String the first set of beads onto the 18-gauge wire. Make a spiral. Attach the 24-gauge wire by coiling it several times around the 18-gauge wire on one side of the focal bead. With chainnose pliers, tuck in the end.

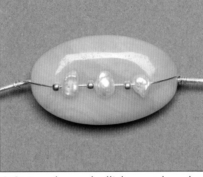

2 String the embellishment beads on the 24-gauge wire and coil the wire again on the other side of the focal bead. Tuck the end.

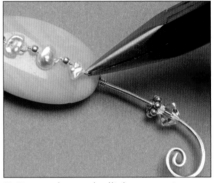

3 Grasp the embellishment wire with chainnose pliers and twist the pliers gently to form small Z shapes. This will tighten the wire to hold the beads in place. String the third set of beads onto the 18-gauge wire. Make a loop, then continue as in steps 5–8 of the Basic Pin to make the stem and catch.

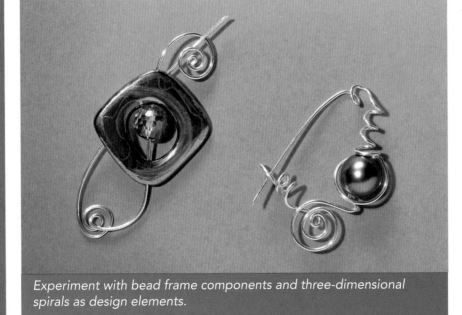

Experiment with bead frame components and three-dimensional spirals as design elements.

50

ZIGZAG WHIMSICAL PIN

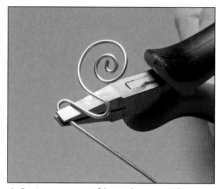

1 String a set of beads onto the 18-gauge wire. (I used a crystal, a spacer, a focal bead, a spacer, and a crystal.) Make a spiral and then zigzag the wire with flatnose pliers.

2 Hammer the spiral and the zigzag with the flat face of the chasing hammer.

3 Add texture using the rounded end of the hammer. Slide the beads to the zigzag and make a zigzag on the other side of the bead set. Make a loop, then continue as in steps 5–8 of the Basic Pin to make the stem and catch.

Try binding the beads to the wire (technique shown in the Spiral Cuff project, page 103).

Celestial Gems

This project shows how easy it is to modify a purchased component for your designs. By making indentations with a small file, you can create a frame for a galaxy of beads on wire.

You'll need

Materials

35 in. (89cm) 24-gauge, dead-soft wire

4 2-in. (51mm) 24-gauge head pins

Strand 4mm freshwater pearls

Assorted 2–14mm pearls, gemstone beads, and crystals

Assorted seed beads

2 earring wires

Large frame, 1⅝ in. (41mm) diam.

2 small frames, 1⅛ in. (29mm) diam.

Tube bail

Hook

2 in. (51mm) extender chain

Open jump ring

Flexible beading wire

2 crimps

Tools and supplies

Chainnose pliers

Roundnose pliers

Flatnose pliers

Side cutters

Flexible beading wire cutters

Crimping pliers

Mini file set

Ruler

Fine-tip permanent marker

This is a good project for the random beads in your collection. It looks wonderful in shades of the same color or in a burst of different colors.

Select beads intuitively. Showcase focal beads by highlighting them with smaller beads on either side.

TO MAKE THE NECKLACE

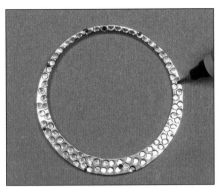

1 Make eight equidistant marks on the silver frame with a fine-tip permanent marker (see **fig. 1**).

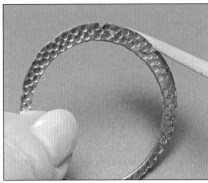

2 Using a double half-round file, make an indentation at each mark.

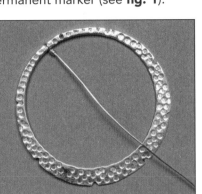

3 To embellish the frame with beads, follow **fig. 1**. Attach about 20 in. (51cm) of wire to the frame at point A with a wrapped loop.

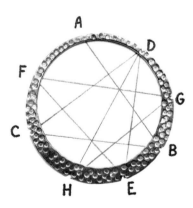

fig. 1

4 String enough beads to fill the space between point A and point B (use larger beads, as this group will be on the front of the pendant). Wrap the wire once tightly around the frame at point B, starting at the front and ending on the back of the frame.

5 Continue stringing beads: String the next group of beads from point B to point C. Use smaller beads, as this group will be on the back of the pendant. Follow **fig. 1** until you get to point D the second time (from point H to point D).

6 Attach the wire at point D with a tight wrapped loop. Tuck in the end with chainnose pliers.

7 String a set of beads on a head pin. Attach it to the hole at the bottom of the frame with a wrapped loop. Attach the frame to the tube bail with a jump ring.

8 To finish the necklace, center the pendant on flexible beading wire and string freshwater pearls on each side until you reach the desired length. Finish with a hook and extender chain. Embellish the extender chain with a wrapped-loop pearl dangle.

TO MAKE THE EARRINGS

Make mirror-image matching earrings in the same way you made the pendant, using the remaining wire (about 15 in./38cm), the smaller frames, and smaller beads.

Make corresponding beaded segments on both earring frames at the same time so they'll be identical. Attach earring wires to the top holes and finish with a wrapped-loop crystal in the bottom holes.

You can make your own frame out of wire!

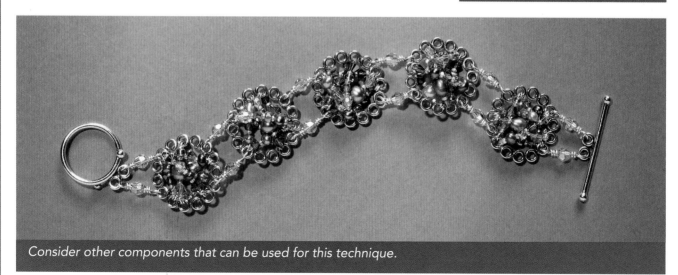

Consider other components that can be used for this technique.

necklace

Wire-wrapped Heart

Wire-wrapping is a popular technique of working with stones that don't have a hole drilled through them. While this wrap is unique to the shape of this stone, the technique can be easily modified to fit many different shapes.

You'll need

Materials

20–24 in. (51–61cm) 24-gauge, dead-soft wire
6 in. (15cm) 22-gauge, half-hard wire
1½ x 1¼ in. (38 x 32mm) focal gemstone heart
Hook
2 cones
2 in. (51mm) extender chain
2 1½-in. (38mm), 24-gauge head pins
2 14–18 in. (36–46cm) pieces of silk string,
    in 2 colors
Assorted 3–5mm crystals and pearls

Tools and supplies

Chainnose pliers
Roundnose pliers
Flatnose pliers
Side cutters
Ruler

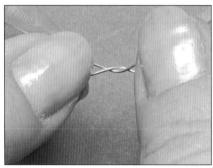

1 Cut the 24-gauge wire in half. Starting about 1 in. (26mm) from the center of each wire, twist the two pieces together.

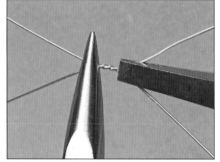

2 Twist three or four times and tighten using flatnose and chainnose pliers.

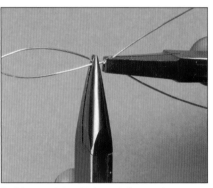

3 About 1 in. (26mm) from the previous twist, twist in the opposite direction two times. Tighten the second twist using flatnose and chainnose pliers.

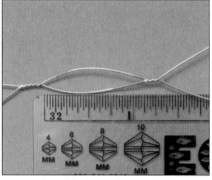

4 You should have about a 1¼-in. (32mm) space between the twists; this should be the centerpoint of both wires.

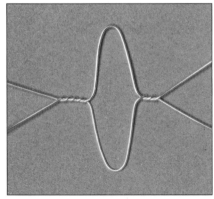

5 Move the twists closer, bending the wire as shown.

6 Insert the heart gemstone between the twists, with the smaller of the two twists in the front.

7 Pull the front wires to the back (inner pair of wires as shown) and the back wires to the front (outer pair).

8 Using chainnose pliers, bend the outer wires upward.

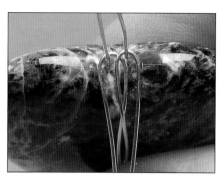

9 Bend each of the inner wires to make a "U-turn" around each outer wire.

10 Grasp the outer wires with chainnose pliers and use flatnose pliers to twist the wires together for about ½ in. (13mm).

11 Use roundnose pliers to form a loop with the twist. This is the bail.

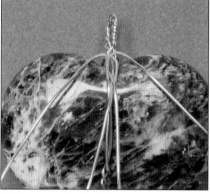

12 Secure the bail by wrapping each of the wire ends around to the front.

13 Bring the ends of the inside pair of wires to the front by going around the back.

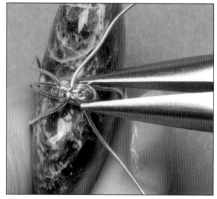

14 Tighten with chainnose pliers.

15 Make soft Z shapes to tighten the wires on the front and the back of the stone.

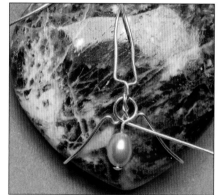

16 Add a wrapped-loop bead unit to the front twist.

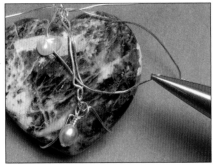

17 String beads on the four wire ends. This part of the wirework is free-form; weave the wire in, out, and around beads.

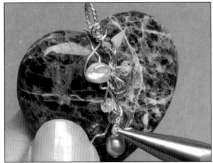

18 Either conceal the wire ends in the wirework or use chainnose pliers to finish the ends with tiny spirals.

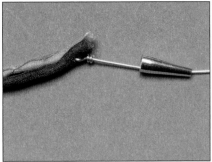

19 String both pieces of silk string through the bail. On both ends, begin a wrapped loop and pierce the ends of the silk with the wire end. Finish wrapping the loop and string a cone onto the wire.

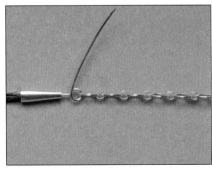

20 On one end, begin another wrapped loop and attach the extender chain.

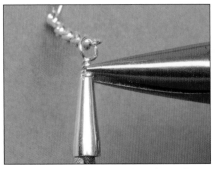

21 Finish the loop and tuck in the end. Attach a wrapped-loop pearl dangle to the end of the extender chain. Connect a hook to the other end with a wrapped loop.

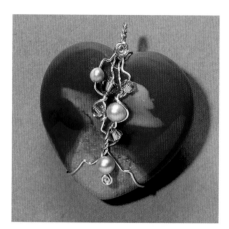

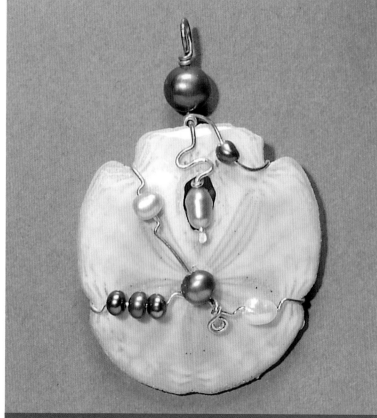

You'll find many ways of adapting this technique to fit all kinds of stones, fossils, or found objects. It may be the answer for showcasing that odd-shaped piece you've had forever!

hook, toggle clasp, and earring wires

Wire Findings

Create custom findings to complement elements in
your necklace, bracelet, or earring designs.

You'll need

Materials

Hook/necklace

2 in. (51mm) 20-gauge, half-hard wire

44–60 in. (112–152cm) 22-gauge, half-hard wire

7 in. (18cm) chain

12–15 3mm round crystals

12–15 4mm round crystals

2 in. (51mm) extender chain

Pendant (I used a sterling silver pendant by artist Russell Smith)

22-gauge head pin

Toggle clasp/bracelet

5 in. (13cm) 20-gauge, half-hard wire

18–24 in. (46–61cm) 22-gauge, half-hard wire

2–2½ in. (51–64mm) chain

12 3mm round crystals

5–7 4mm round crystals

3 12mm cosmic-cut crystals

Ear wires/earrings

7 in. (18cm) 20-gauge, half-hard wire

2 2mm silver rounds

2 4mm round crystals

2 12mm cosmic-cut crystals

Tools and supplies

Chainnose pliers

Roundnose pliers

Flatnose pliers

Side cutters

Small stepped wire-wrapping pliers

Bench block

Chasing hammer

Cup bur

Ruler

Liver of sulfur (optional)

TO MAKE THE HOOK CLASP (NECKLACE)

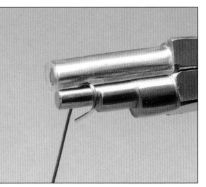

1 About ½ in. (13mm) from the wire end, bend the 20-gauge wire into a hook using the first step of the wire-wrapping pliers.

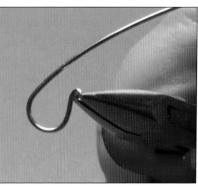

2 Using chainnose pliers, bend the end of the wire into a tiny U.

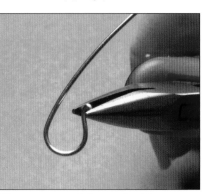

3 Squeeze to tighten the U.

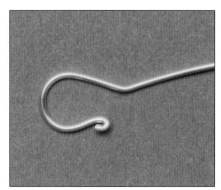

4 Using flatnose pliers, make a slight bend opposite the U.

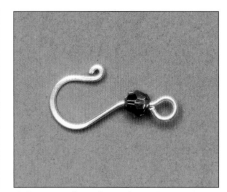

5 Place the piece on the bench block and hammer only the curved section to flatten.

6 String a bead on the wire and make a basic loop.

7 Finish the necklace using 22-gauge wire; center the pendant and connect beaded wrapped loops and chain links. Attach the hook to one end and the extender chain to the other, finishing with a wrapped-loop bead unit. Use liver of sulfur to add patina if desired.

TO MAKE THE TOGGLE CLASP (BRACELET)

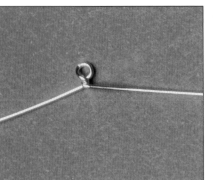

1 Cut 2 in. (51mm) of 20-gauge wire. With roundnose pliers, make a loop in the center. Grasp the loop with flatnose pliers and make several twists below the loop.

2 String five 3mm crystals on each side of the twist. Make a small spiral on each end.

3 Cut a 3-in. (76mm) piece of 20-gauge wire. Wrap it once around the largest step on the wire-wrapping pliers, leaving one end longer than the other. The short end should be at least 5/16 in. (8mm).

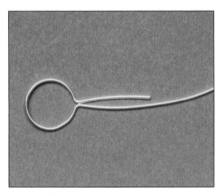

4 Use flatnose pliers to bend the ends of the wires so that they are parallel to each other.

5 Hammer the ring lightly to flatten it.

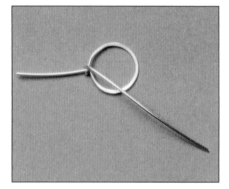

6 Wrap the long end once around the base of the short end.

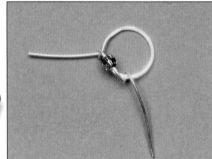

7 String a bead on the long end of the wire. Wrap the wire around the side of the ring.

9 Use 22-gauge wire to finish the bracelet using beaded wrapped-loop units and chain links. Attach the toggle clasp and add patina if desired.

8 Make a loop in the short end. Wrap the long end around the ring several times and tuck in the end.

TO MAKE THE EARRINGS

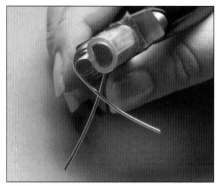

1 Wrap 2½ in. (64mm) of 20-gauge wire around the second step of the wire-wrapping pliers and bend the wire so the ends cross.

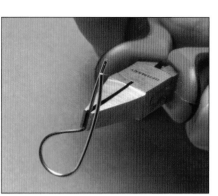

2 Using the flatnose pliers, bend one side of the wire so that it is parallel to the other side.

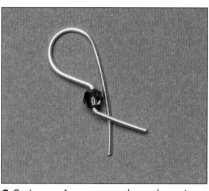

3 String a 4mm crystal on the wire. Bend the end so it crosses the other wire end.

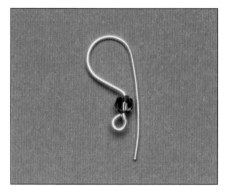

4 Make a loop below the crystal.

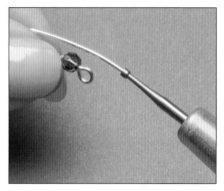

5 Smooth the end of the earring wire with the cup bur.

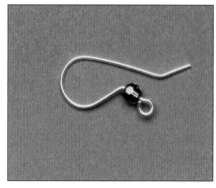

6 Using flatnose pliers, angle the end of the wire. Repeat steps 1–6 to make the other earring wire.

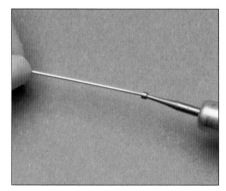

7 Cut two 1-in. (26mm) lengths of 20-gauge wire for the head-pin bead units. Round one end of each with the cup bur.

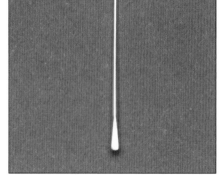

8 Hammer the rounded ends into a paddle.

9 String a 2mm silver bead and a 12mm crystal on each head pin. Connect them to the earring wires with a loop. Add patina if desired.

To create sturdy clasps, use 20-gauge wire or thicker.

63

Why settle for the same old earring wires and closures? Create a stylish look of your own using the Wire Findings techniques.

Zigzag Rings

In this set of projects, you'll learn ring-sizing techniques as you create playful wire rings that are sturdy enough for everyday wear.

You'll need

Materials

Basic Zigzag Ring

5–7 in. (13–18cm) 16-gauge, half-hard wire

2 in. (51mm) 24-gauge, half-hard wire

14mm focal bead

Crystal Burst Zigzag Ring

5–7 in. (13–18cm) 16-gauge, half-hard wire

3 in. (76mm) 24-gauge, half-hard wire

40–50 2mm sterling silver rounds

40–50 4mm bicone crystals

40–50 1½-in. (38mm), 24-gauge head pins

Art Bead Zigzag Ring

7–9 in. (18–23cm) 16-gauge, half-hard wire

Art bead (I used a bead by artist Jeff Plath)

Tools and supplies

Chainnose pliers

Roundnose pliers

Flatnose pliers

Side cutters

Bench block

Chasing hammer

Ring mandrel

Ruler

Self-stick notes

As you bend and hammer the wire, your ring will become sturdier. There is a limit, however; too much work-hardening can make wire brittle and prone to breakage.

BASIC ZIGZAG RING

1 To determine your ring size, wrap a self-stick note around your finger and make a mark at one full wrap. If you know your size, work directly on the mandrel at the correct size.

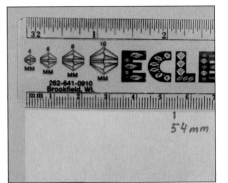

2 Measure this distance in millimeters for precision. (My size-7 ring measured 54mm.) Subtract the length of the focal bead plus 2mm from the total ring measurement to get the length of your wire component. (My wire component was 38mm.)

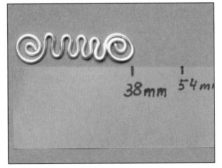

3 Using flatnose pliers and the 16-gauge wire, make a loose spiral on one end.

4 Using flatnose pliers, make zigzags until the wire component is approximately one-spiral-width less than the desired length.

5 Cut the straight wire end to approximately 1½ in. (38mm) and shape a second spiral. Check that your component is the desired length and adjust if necessary.

6 Place the wire component on the bench block and hammer it, flattening it slightly.

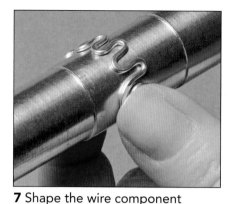

7 Shape the wire component around the mandrel.

8 If necessary, continue to curve the shape with flatnose pliers.

9 Check the fit on the mandrel, allowing room for the focal bead.

10 Wrap 24-gauge wire around the side of one spiral.

11 String the bead on the wire, finish wrapping the wire around the side of the other spiral, and tuck in the wire ends.

CRYSTAL BURST ZIGZAG RING

1 Follow steps 1–9 of the Basic Zigzag Ring. Make 40–50 wire-wrapped crystal components using 4mm bicones and 2mm silver rounds on head pins.

2 Wrap 24-gauge wire twice around the side of one spiral, string half of the wrapped-loop components, wrap twice around the side of the other spiral, and string the remaining components on the wire. Wrap twice around the side of the first spiral and tuck in the wire ends.

ART BEAD ZIGZAG RING

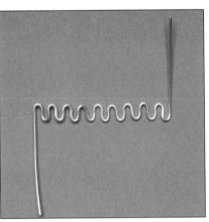

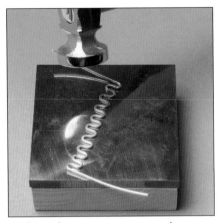

1 Determine the ring size in millimeters as for the Basic Zigzag Ring. Using flatnose pliers, make zigzags in the 16-gauge wire until the component reaches the ring size length. Trim the straight wire ends to 1½ in. (38mm).

2 Place the component on the bench block and hammer only the zigzag section to flatten; do not hammer the straight sections.

3 Shape the wire component around the mandrel using flatnose pliers until the ring is the desired size. Bend the straight ends of the wire as shown.

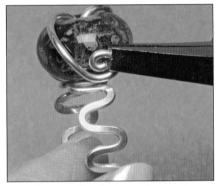

4 String both straight ends through the bead and shape the wires around the bead to hold it.

5 Make small spirals at the ends of both wires toward the back of the bead.

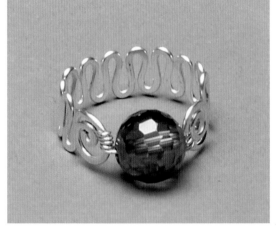

Many fresh designs can flow from the Zigzag Rings techniques! Use two wires for a two-holed bead such as the eye bead below.

pendant

Wire-wrapped Donut

Large donuts have a lot of surface, making them a nice backdrop for wire embellishment. Highlight the special colors and textures of a donut with complementary beads.

You'll need

Materials

18–24 in. (46–61cm) 18-gauge, dead-soft wire
10–12 in. (25–31cm) 24-gauge, dead-soft wire
Gemstone donut, 1½–2 in. (38–51mm) diam.
Assorted 3–8mm pearls, gemstone beads,
   and crystals

Tools and supplies

Chainnose pliers
Roundnose pliers
Flatnose pliers
Side cutters
Small stepped wire-wrapping pliers
Ruler

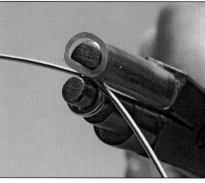

1 On the first step of the wire-wrapping pliers, make a bail from the 18-gauge wire. Work from the center of the wire and make two complete turns.

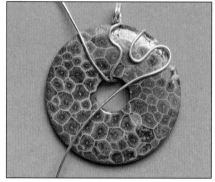

2 Using flatnose pliers, make a soft 90° bend in both wires.

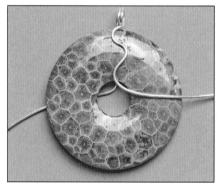

3 Using chainnose or flatnose pliers, make soft zigzags or curves in both wires until you reach the opening of the donut.

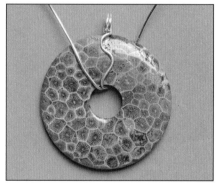

4 String both ends of the wire through the opening of the donut.

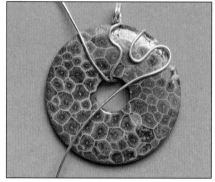

5 Use roundnose pliers to create U-turns and S-bends in the wire as you continue to wrap around the donut. Occasionally string the wire through the donut opening to hold the donut securely.

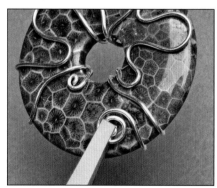

6 After wrapping the entire donut, bring the wire ends to the front of the piece. Make a spiral at the end of each wire, leaving a ³⁄₁₆–⁵⁄₁₆ in. (5–8mm) gap between the spirals.

7 Wrap 24-gauge wire around one of the spirals several times and tuck in the end. String a bead, attach the wire to the second spiral, trim the wire, and tuck in the end.

8 Continue embellishing by wire-wrapping beads to the front.

Use this technique wherever you want to use donuts—for bracelets and pins as well as pendants.

necklace, bracelet, and earrings

Framed Pearls

This project has a very clean and contemporary
look. The wire setting elegantly frames the pearls,
almost like a bezel.

TO MAKE THE BRACELET

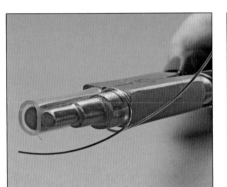

1 On the third step of the wire-wrapping pliers, shape a ring with the 22-gauge square wire.

2 Wrap slightly more than 1½ times around the tool to make a frame.

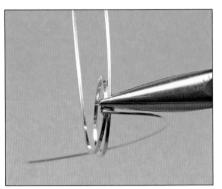

3 Wrap one end of the 24-gauge wire three times around one side of the frame. Use chainnose pliers to tighten the wrap.

You'll need

Materials

24–30 in. (61–76cm) 22-gauge, half-hard, square wire
12–15 in. (31–38cm) 24-gauge, dead-soft wire
8–10 in. (20–25cm) large-link chain
6–8 in. (15–20cm) large-link chain
4 links of large-link chain (for earrings)
Lobster claw clasp
22-gauge head pin
11 open jump rings
Toggle clasp
2 earring wires
10–12 14mm shell pearls
4mm silver rounds

Tools and supplies

Chainnose pliers
Roundnose pliers
Flatnose pliers
Side cutters
Small stepped wire-wrapping pliers
Ruler

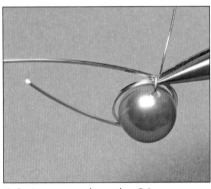

4 String a pearl on the 24-gauge wire. Wrap the wire three times on the other side of the frame going in the opposite direction. Trim the wire and tuck in the end.

5 Trim the straight ends of the square wire to approximately ³⁄₁₆ in. (5mm).

Choose pearls of the same size for the best results.

6 Working near the tip of the roundnose pliers, make a tiny loop on each side of the frame.

7 For a 7-in. (18cm) bracelet, make 7 framed pearl components and connect them with jump rings. Connect the toggle loop to one end with a jump ring and use at least three rings to connect the toggle bar.

TO MAKE THE NECKLACE

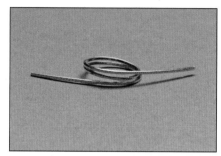

1 Repeat steps 1–6 of the bracelet instructions to make one framed-pearl component. Attach one length of large-link chain to each side (one side will be longer than the other).

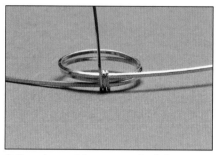

2 Connect the lobster claw clasp to the shorter end with a jump ring. String a 4mm bead on a head pin and attach it to the longer end with a wrapped loop.

TO MAKE THE EARRINGS

1 Use the third step of the wire-wrapping pliers to make a ring with the 22-gauge square wire. Wrap again to make two complete rings.

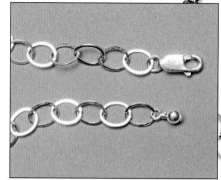

2 Starting with one end of the 24-gauge wire, wrap around the overlap three times.

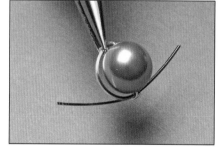

3 String a pearl on the 24-gauge wire. Wrap the wire three times on the other side going in the opposite direction, trim, and tuck in the end with chainnose pliers.

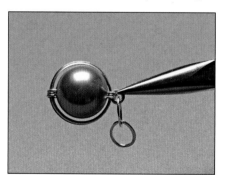

4 Trim the ends of the square wire, leaving approximately ³⁄₁₆ in. (5mm). The wire ends point in opposite directions; working with one end at a time, roll a tiny loop back over the wraps so the two loops function as one. Attach a two-link chain as you form the loops.

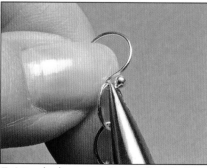

5 Attach the ear wire to the chain. Repeat to make a second earring.

This pea pod frame was shaped from a single piece of wire.

Coil fine-gauge wire all around the frame.

Frame a favorite focal bead (this bead is by Green Girl Studios).

framed pin

Beaded Leaf

Making this stylized leaf pin is a great way to play with a nature-inspired color palette on a miniature scale.

You'll need

Materials
20–24 in. (51–61cm) 18-gauge, half-hard wire
5–6 ft. (1.5–2m) 24-gauge, dead-soft wire
130–150 assorted 3–6mm crystals and pearls

Tools and supplies
Chainnose pliers
Roundnose pliers
Flatnose pliers
Side cutters
Bench block
Chasing hammer
Sharpening stone
Ruler

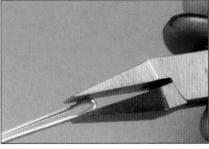

1 Bend the 18-gauge wire in half and squeeze the bend with flatnose pliers to make the point of the leaf.

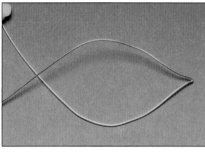

2 Use your fingers to shape a simple leaf form approximately 3 in. (76mm) long.

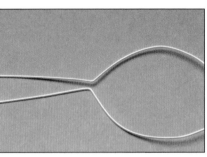

3 Use flatnose pliers to bend the ends of the wire at sharp angles so they are parallel to each other.

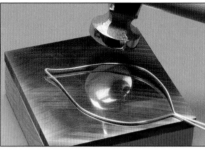

4 Hammer the leaf shape to flatten the wire, avoiding the straight sections.

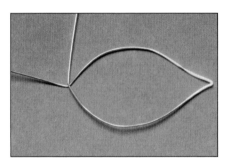

5 Bend one of the straight sections so it is perpendicular to the other.

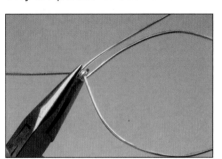

6 Wrap the bent wire around the straight wire several times. Tighten the wrap with chainnose pliers.

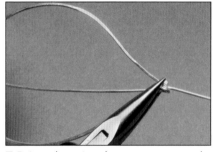

7 Bring the wire that you wrapped toward the tip of the leaf. Wrap it several times around the tip and tighten the wrap.

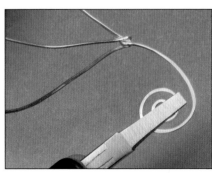

8 Trim the wire to 3 in. (76mm) and make a spiral. Hammer the spiral to flatten it slightly.

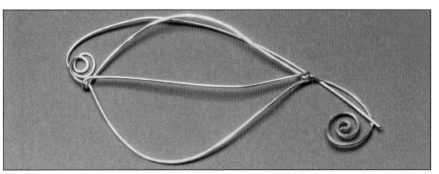

9 Use roundnose pliers to start a spiral at the other end, facing the opposite direction of the first spiral. Continue making a loop with your fingers, gently shaping the remaining wire toward the first spiral on the other end. Shape the loop toward the back of the leaf so that the pin wire falls behind the leaf. Pin the wire on the spiral hook and trim to approximately ¼ in. (7mm) past the hook.

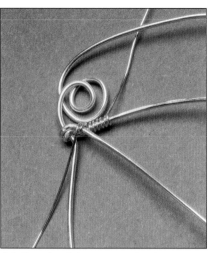

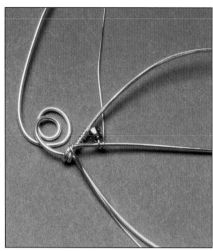

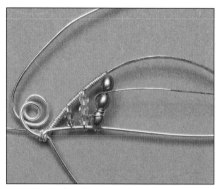

12 Wrap the frame 5–10 times. (Wrap 10–15 times if you like wider gaps between beaded segments.) Continue wrapping and adding beaded segments to fill one side of the leaf shape, occasionally spiraling the wire around larger beads on its return to the frame. Secure the wire by wrapping it around the frame tightly. Trim and tuck the wire end.

10 Cut the 24-gauge wire into a comfortable length (between 18–36 in./46–91cm). Wrap the wire end around the leaf frame near the second spiral 5–10 times.

11 String beads to fill the gap between the center wire and the frame. Wrap the wire around the center wire twice and bring the wire around the frame from the back.

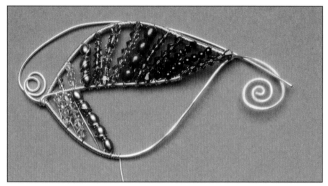

13 The wire coils you made around the center wire will help anchor the new beaded segments. Continue adding segments until the second half of the leaf is full.

14 Sharpen the wire end and lightly hammer the pin to work-harden.

Using this technique with different colors of seed beads of the same size will give you an entirely different look. Try it!

Experiment with different types of leaf shapes and other designs. Try spacing the beads close together.

pendant

Wire-wrapped Cabochon

Wire-wrapping a cabochon is a great alternative to a traditionally fabricated bezel. No torch or solder is required!

You'll need

Materials

30 in. (76cm) 22-gauge, half-hard, square wire

10–12 in. (25–31cm) 22-gauge, half-hard, half-round wire

Gemstone cabochon, about 2 in. (51mm) long

Tools and supplies

Chainnose pliers

Roundnose pliers

Flatnose pliers

Side cutters

Large stepped wire-wrapping pliers

Pin vise

Fine-tip permanent marker

Ruler

A cabochon (sometimes shortened to "cab") is a flat-backed gemstone that is highly polished but not faceted.

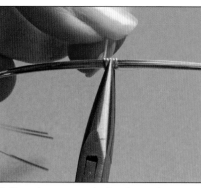

1 Cut the square wire into three equal pieces and align them. Use the half-round wire to wrap them tightly in the center a minimum of five times.

2 Tuck the wire to the inside of the wrap so that it will be concealed by the stone.

3 Use the stepped wire-wrapping pliers to curve the center of the wire.

4 Continue shaping until the outline follows the shape of the bottom and sides of the cabochon.

5 Make wraps on each side of the wire outline with half-round wire. Wrap at least three times (symmetry is optional!).

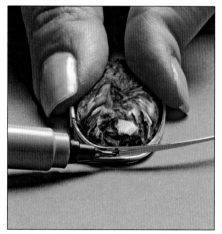

6 Shape the top of the outline around the top of the cabochon; it must fit the cab very closely. Use a permanent marker to mark the intersection of the two sets of wire.

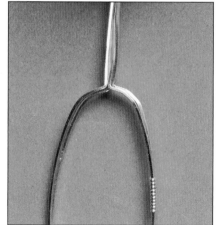

7 Use flatnose pliers to bend the two sets of wire upward at the marks so they run parallel to each other.

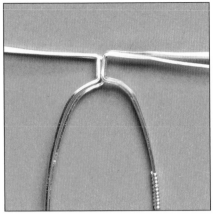

8 Use flatnose pliers to bend the wires at right angles approximately ⅜ in. (10mm) above the previous bend to create a neck.

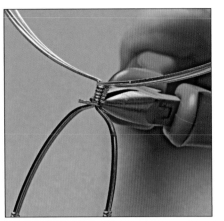

9 Wrap the neck with half-round wire. Use chainnose pliers to tighten the top and bottom wraps against the neck.

10 Trim the ends of the half-round wire as shown.

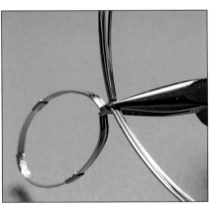

11 Use chainnose pliers to tuck the top end upward and the bottom end under the neck.

12 Place a square wire end in the pin vise and twist. Hold the neck steady with chainnose pliers while twisting.

13 Twist all six square wire ends, one at a time. Keep the wires separated in two groups of three.

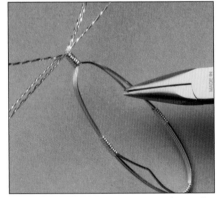

14 Use flatnose pliers to make soft bends in wire on the front of the bezel.

15 Insert the cabochon.

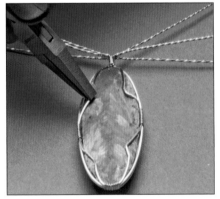

16 Make soft bends in the back wire.

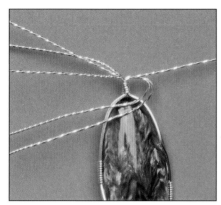

17 Pair the second and third twisted wires on one side of the neck. Bring them over the front of the cabochon in a soft wave.

18 Bend them around toward the back and wrap them around one of the bent wires on the back.

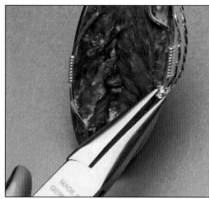

19 Trim and tuck in the ends.

20 Pair the second and third wires on the opposite side of the neck and curve them to the back in a soft wave. Wrap them around a back wire and trim.

21 Trim the remaining two wires to ½ in. (13mm).

22 Use roundnose pliers to make a loop in each wire for the bail. Trim and tuck the ends close to the neck.

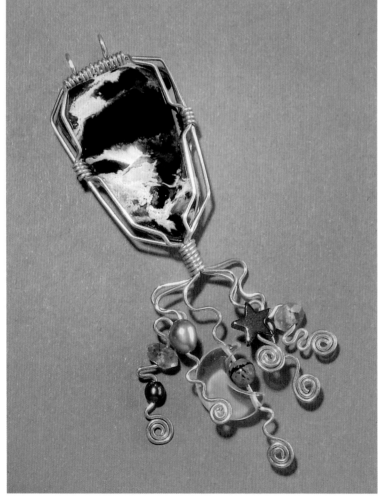

You can bezel a faceted gemstone in the same way. Capture two stones by using more wire. Extra wire can also be embellished with beads.

pendant

Wire-wrapped Stone

You can choose a smaller or unusually shaped stone for this project and give it substance by building a frame around it.

You'll need

Materials

5 in. (13mm) 20-gauge, half-hard wire

16–20 in. (41–51cm) 22-gauge, half-hard, square wire

Gemstone cabochon, approximately 1⅝ in. (41mm) long

24-gauge, 1½ in. (38mm) head pin

8 x 10mm freshwater pearl

Tools and Supplies

Chainnose pliers

Roundnose pliers

Flatnose pliers

Side cutters

Pin vise

Ruler

This technique works best with long cabochons.

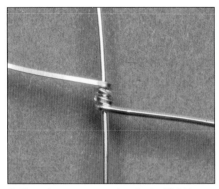

1 Cut the square wire in half. Wrap one piece around the round wire, starting in the center of both wires. Wrap three to five times. Finish with the ends pointing in opposite directions.

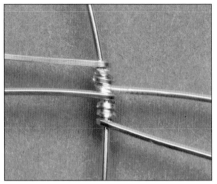

2 Below the first wire, repeat step 1 using the second piece of square wire.

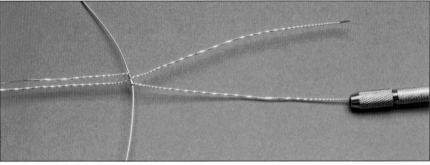

3 Place each of the four square wires in the pin vise and twist. Hold the opposite end with chainnose pliers while twisting.

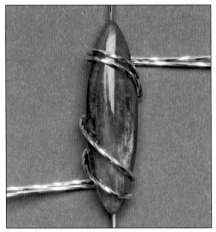

4 Center the stone cabochon over the vertical wire. Holding the stone firmly, pair the wires on each side, and wrap each pair once around the front, ending in back.

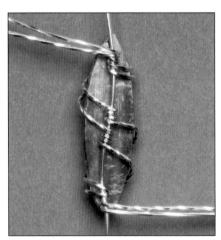

5 Use chainnose pliers to wrap each pair around the center back wire tightly.

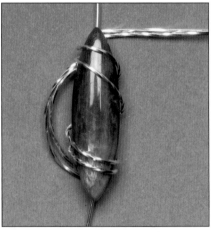

6 Curve the bottom pair of wires upward in back to frame the stone. Wrap the wires around the center wire in back of the stone.

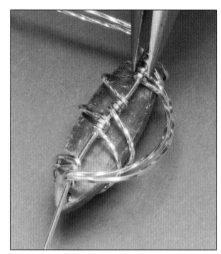

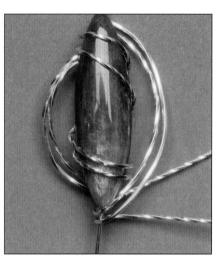

7 Trim the pair of wires just wrapped. Tuck in the ends using chainnose pliers.

8 Curve the top pair of wires downward in front. Wrap both wires around the center wire below the stone.

9 Wrap several times, trim the wires, and tuck in the ends.

10 In the vertical wire at the top, make a wrapped loop perpendicular to the stone for the bail.

11 Make a wrapped loop at the base of the stone. Attach a wrapped-loop pearl dangle to the loop.

Do you prefer a more modern look? These variations use 16-gauge, half-round wire.

Celtic Knots

Interlocking knots is a design device common to many cultures, including Celtic and Asian traditions. By changing the bead selection and color scheme, you can bring a different ethnic flair to your piece.

You'll need

Materials

Bracelet

18–24 in. (46–61cm) 22-gauge, half-hard wire
14–20 in. (36–51cm) 18-gauge, dead-soft wire
8–10 4mm round gemstone beads
Purchased or handmade toggle clasp

Necklace

8 in. (20cm) 24-gauge, dead-soft wire
30–36 in. (76–91cm) 22-gauge, half-hard wire
10–12 in. (25–31cm) 16-gauge, dead-soft wire
2 in. (51mm) extender chain
22-gauge, 1½-in. (38mm) head pin
2 open jump rings
Purchased or handmade hook clasp
13–17 4mm gemstone beads
2 8mm large-hole gemstone beads
Leaf pendant (I used a porcelain pendant by
    Melanie Brooks, Earthenwood Studio)

Earrings

4 in. (10cm) 24-gauge, dead-soft wire
8–10 in. (20–25cm) 18-gauge, dead-soft wire
2 earring wires
2 24-gauge, 1½-in. (38mm) head pins
2 soldered jump rings
2 16mm teardrop gemstone beads

Tools and supplies

Chainnose pliers
Roundnose pliers
Flatnose pliers
Side cutters
Small stepped wire-wrapping pliers
Bench block
Chasing hammer
Ruler

 You can make your own closures from 18-gauge wire (see Wire Findings, page 60). I used a toggle clasp on the bracelet and a hook clasp on the necklace.

TO MAKE THE BRACELET

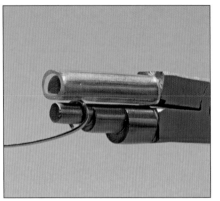

1 Using the 18-gauge wire, make the large side of a figure-eight component on the first step of the wire-wrapping pliers.

2 Use roundnose pliers to make the small side, looping the wire in the opposite direction.

3 Hammer the component to flatten it. Repeat steps 1–3 until you have 14–18 components (7–9 pairs).

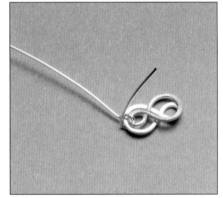

4 Slide a gemstone bead onto the 22-gauge wire and begin a wrapped loop. Slide two figure-eight components into the loop with the components facing in opposite direction. Wrap the loop.

5 Continue connecting figure-eight pairs and beaded wrapped-loop links. Attach half of the toggle clasp to a wrapped-loop link on each end.

TO MAKE THE NECKLACE

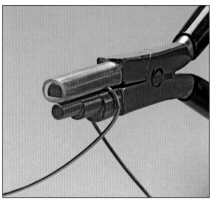

1 On the third step of the wire-wrapping pliers, bend the 16-gauge wire into a teardrop shape.

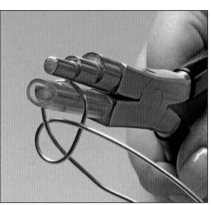

2 Use the wire-wrapping pliers to bend one end into a teardrop shape the same size as the first (the two teardrops will overlap in the center).

3 String the end of the wire through the center from the opposite direction. If the wire kinks, you may need to use flatnose pliers to round it out gently.

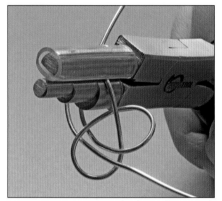

4 Repeat step 2 with the other end of the wire.

5 Repeat step 3 to create a trefoil shape.

6 Gently hammer the component to harden, not flatten, it, using very little force on the wire intersections.

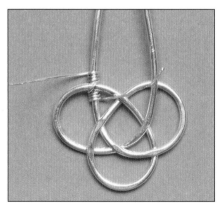

7 Bind the intersecting wires with 24-gauge wire, starting in the center of the wire and making 3–4 coils at each intersection.

8 Make small spirals in each end of the wire and bend them to conceal the coils.

9 String a bead onto each of the 16-gauge wire ends and curve the ends symmetrically using roundnose pliers. Make a loop on each end.

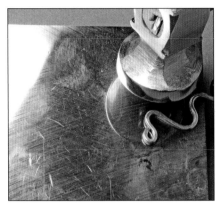

10 Gently hammer the curved sections, avoiding the beads.

11 Make 24 figure-eight components (12 pairs) using 18-gauge wire. Connect them to the trefoil component using beaded wrapped-loop links as in the bracelet instructions.

12 Attach the hook to one end and the extender chain to the other with wrapped-loop links. String a bead on a head pin and attach it to the end of the extender chain with a wrapped loop.

13 Use two jump rings to attach the porcelain leaf to the trefoil component.

TO MAKE THE EARRINGS

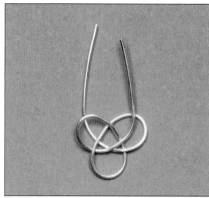

1 Repeat steps 1–5 from the necklace directions.

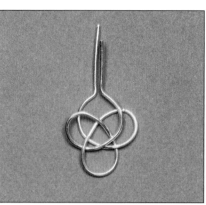

2 Using flatnose pliers, shape the two wire ends so they are parallel.

3 Use a 2-in. (51mm) piece of 24-gauge wire to make 3–4 coils around the wires. End with a small spiral and bend it to conceal the coils.

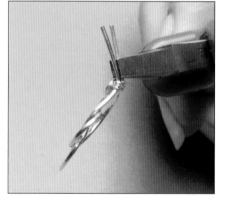

4 Cut the wire ends to approximately ½ in. (13mm) and bend them in a right angle.

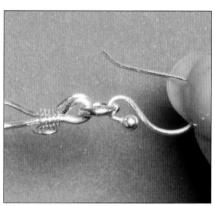

5 Make loops in both ends, slide a jump ring into both loops, and close the loops. Attach an ear wire to the jump ring.

6 String a bead on a head pin, and attach it to the earring base with a wrapped loop. Repeat steps 1–6 to make a second earring.

Once you master forming the knots in wire, have fun bringing different beads and pendants into the mix. The handmade porcelain square is from Clay River Designs.

Leaf Silhouettes

This design unites elements from earlier projects, reinterpreting them in heavy-gauge wire. The focus here is on the wire shapes, each with substantial textured surface area.

You'll need

Materials

5–6 ft. (1.5–1.8m) 16-gauge, dead-soft wire

2 earring wires

Assorted large-hole gemstone beads

Large-hole spacers

Tools and supplies

Chainnose pliers

Roundnose pliers

Flatnose pliers

Side cutters

Small stepped wire-wrapping pliers

Bench block

Chasing hammer

Cup bur

File

Ruler

 It may be helpful to have an actual leaf, or a sketch or photo of a leaf, for reference as you shape this project.

TO MAKE THE NECKLACE

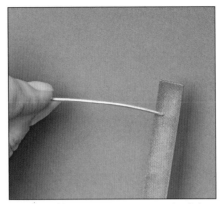

1 Use a file to taper one end of the wire.

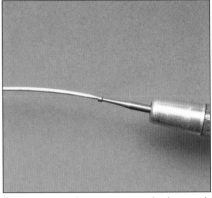

2 Use a cup bur to smooth the end.

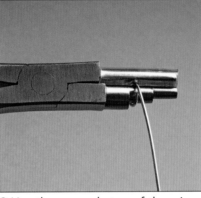

3 Use the second step of the wire-wrapping pliers to shape a two-coil spiral with an open center.

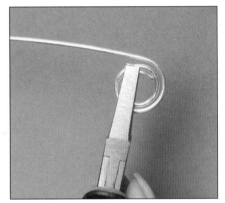

4 Use flatnose pliers to continue shaping past the first coil. Continue until you are past the second coil.

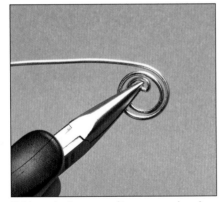

5 Use chainnose pliers to make the loop on the inside of the spiral.

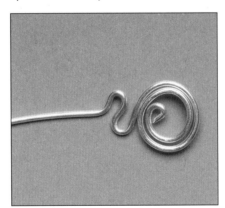

6 Use the flatnose pliers to zigzag the wire as shown.

7 Using the rounded end of the hammer, texture the curved sections of the wire.

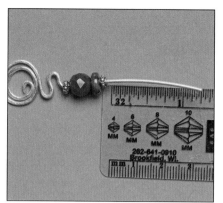

8 String the beads onto the wire. Measure 1¼ in. (32mm) from the last bead and trim the wire.

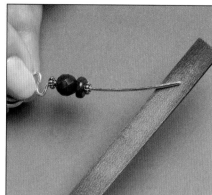

9 Use a file to taper the end of the wire.

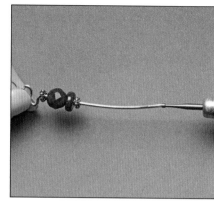

10 Use a cup bur to smooth the end.

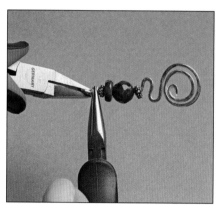

11 At the end, make a wrapped loop perpendicular to the spiral.

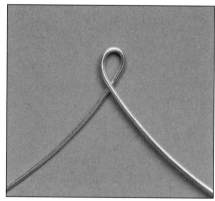

12 Cut a piece of wire 7–9 in. (18–23cm) long, depending on the size of the leaf you want to create. Wrap the center of the wire around one side of the roundnose pliers until it crosses to form a teardrop shape.

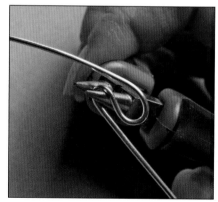

13 Use roundnose pliers to bend the wires upward.

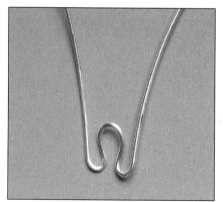

14 Bend the wire on both sides of the teardrop as shown.

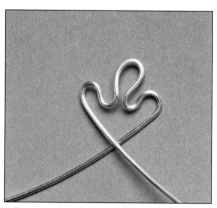

15 Use roundnose pliers on both sides to bend the wires down, forming the top of the oak leaf.

16 Continue shaping the wire in this way until the leaf shape is complete. Bend the wire ends so the are parallel to each other.

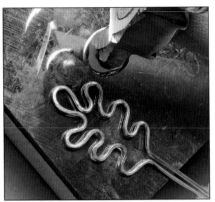

17 Use the rounded end of the hammer to texture the leaf shape, avoiding the straight sections of the wire.

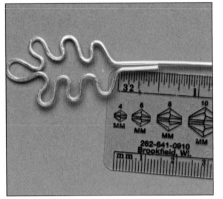

18 Trim one end to ½ in. (13mm).

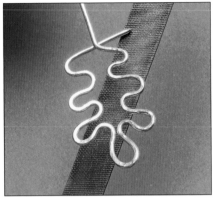

19 Bend the short end to cross the longer wire and file the end.

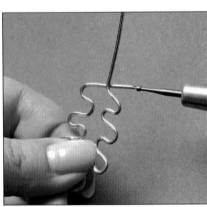

20 Use a cup bur to smooth the end.

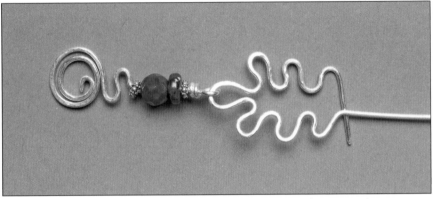

21 Slide the leaf silhouette onto the wrapped loop of the spiral component.

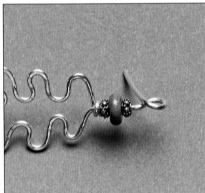

22 Wrap the short wire end around the other wire end at the base of the leaf shape. String the beads onto the wire. File and smooth the wire end. Begin a wrapped loop, leaving it unwrapped so it is ready to connect to the next component.

23 Continue making leaf and spiral components (you may want to make some of them without zigzags). Connect them to make a chain. On one end, leave one loop unwrapped so you can connect the bar in step 28.

24 On the other end, make and attach the ring for the clasp in the same way that you made spiral components, but using a larger step on the wire-wrapping pliers.

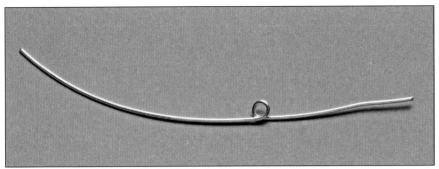

25 To make the bar, make a loop approximately 2 in. (51mm) from the end of the wire. Trim the other end to 2 in. (51mm). File and smooth both ends.

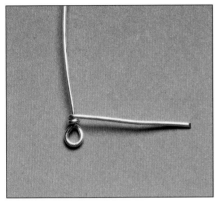

26 Wrap the loop.

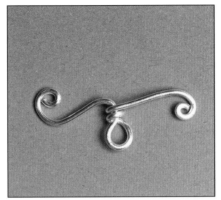

27 Shape and spiral the ends as shown.

28 Hammer the bar, avoiding the wrapped loop. Attach the bar to the unwrapped loop and wrap the loop.

TO MAKE THE EARRINGS

Make two beaded leaf components and attach them to the earring wires.

If you make the leaf silhouettes into a bracelet, give the components a slight curve for a graceful fit.

bracelet

Spiral Cuff

This cuff provides a basic structure that allows your creativity to flow. Feel free to embellish as you like—the design is very adaptable to suit your personal style.

You'll need

Materials

2½–3 ft. (76–91cm) 16-gauge, dead-soft wire

5–6 ft. (1.5–1.8m) 24-gauge, dead-soft wire

Assorted 3–10mm gemstone beads, crystals, and pearls

Tools and supplies

Chainnose pliers

Roundnose pliers

Flatnose pliers

Side cutters

Small stepped wire-wrapping pliers

Large stepped wire-wrapping pliers (or ring mandrel)

Bench block

Chasing hammer

Bracelet mandrel

Twist ties

Ruler

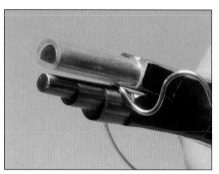

1 Starting in the center of the 16-gauge wire, shape soft waves on the third step of the small wire-wrapping pliers.

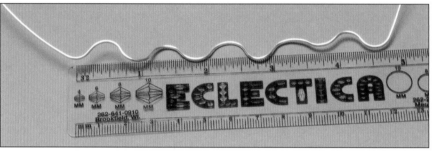

2 Continue making waves until the shape is about 4½ in. (11cm) long.

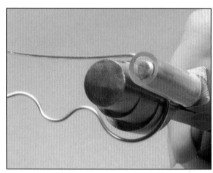

3 Use the third step on the large wire-wrapping pliers (or use a ring mandrel) to shape a 1⅛-in. (29mm) diam. semicircle at each end of the wave shape.

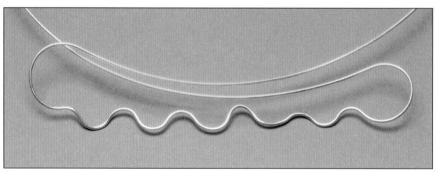

4 Including the semicircles, the shape should be approximately 6 in. (15cm) long.

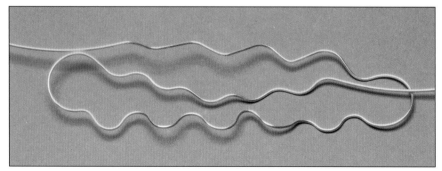

5 Bend both ends of the wire as in step 1, until each wave shape reaches the opposite semicircle.

6 Trim the wire end to 5 in. (13cm) and make a spiral on the end.

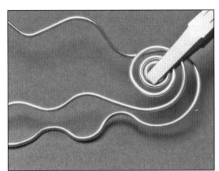

7 Continue shaping with the flatnose pliers, fitting the spiral into the semicircle.

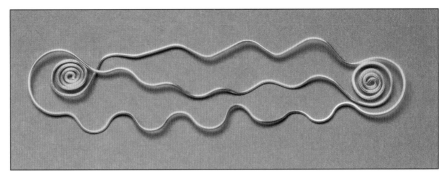

8 Repeat steps 5–7 on the other end.

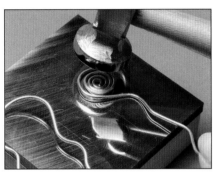

9 Using the flat face of the hammer, flatten the entire shape. Make sure no wires cross while hammering.

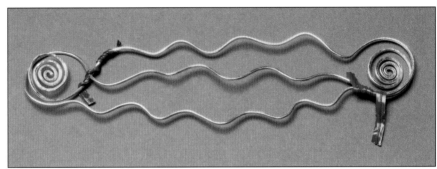

10 Use twist ties to secure the wires as shown.

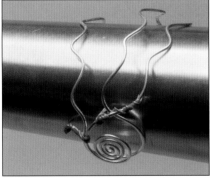

11 Shape the bracelet on a bracelet mandrel. Check the fit.

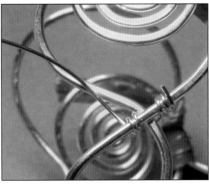

12 Cut the 24-gauge wire to a comfortable working length. Starting at one end of the 24-gauge wire, bind the 16-gauge wire where it intersects.

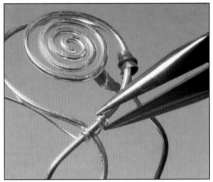

13 Bind until the intersection is secure. Tuck in the wire end with chainnose pliers.

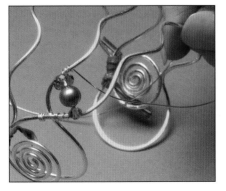

14 String a set of beads on the end of the 24-gauge wire, using a selection of beads that best fits the space between the two wires. Coil the wire 2–3 times to secure.

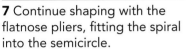

Try 18–36 in. (46–91cm) as a comfortable working length of binding wire. Just coil a few times around the 16-gauge wire to start a new length if you run out.

15 Continue to add beads in this way until you have completed half of the bracelet, removing the twist ties as you work. Trim and tuck in the wire end. Repeat steps 12–14 for the other side of the bracelet. Use 24-gauge wire to bind the outer wire of the spiral to the semicircles, adding beads where space allows. Trim and tuck in the wire ends.

Although this technique makes a beautiful cuff, it has great possibilities for other types of jewelry.

necklace

Window Wrap

This wrap is an elegant solution for securing an undrilled, three-dimensional stone such as a marble or a beach stone. The open wrap allows the beauty of the stone to shine.

You'll need

Materials

30–36 in. (76–91cm) 18-gauge, dead-soft wire
40–46 in. (1–1.2m) 20-gauge, half-hard wire
4 ft. (1.2m) 24-gauge, dead-soft wire
2 x 1⅛ x ⅝ in. (51 x 29 x 16mm) gemstone
Assorted faceted gemstone beads
Hook clasp
2 in. (51mm) extender chain
Sterling silver spacers
22-gauge, 1½-in. (38mm) head pin
15–19 12mm round gemstone beads

Tools and supplies

Chainnose pliers
Roundnose pliers
Side cutters
Large stepped wire-wrapping pliers
Fine-tip permanent marker
Ruler

If you are wrapping a smaller stone, use a smaller gauge of wire.

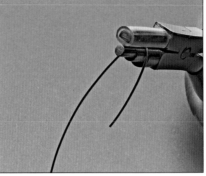

1 Use the second step of the wire-wrapping pliers to make a U shape about 1½ in. (38mm) from the end of the 18-gauge wire. This is the start of the inner frame. Using the stone as a guide in shaping, shape ovals of increasing size until you have circled three times on one side and four times on the other.

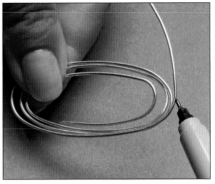

2 Hold the frame tightly in your fingers (at this point it has a lot of spring). Use a fine-tip marker to mark the midpoint of the side with four wires.

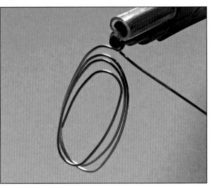

3 Use the first step of the wire-wrapping pliers to make a loop in the outer wire at the mark. Shape the wire to complete the side of the fourth/outer oval opposite the loop. At the point opposite the loop, make a second loop the same size as the first.

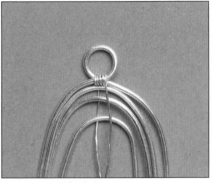

4 Using half of the 24-gauge wire, start in the center of the wire and bind the first loop to the frame by coiling five times.

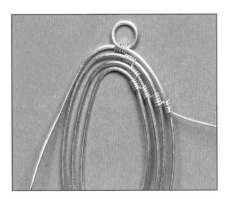

5 Using one end of the 24-gauge wire, coil around the next wire on the frame. Continue moving toward the inside of the frame, wrapping each level as shown, including the innermost wire. Change direction and coil toward the outermost wire.

Repeat steps 4–5 on the opposite side of the frame.

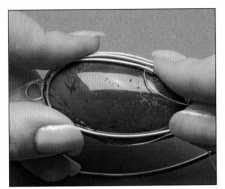

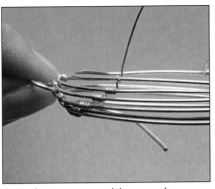

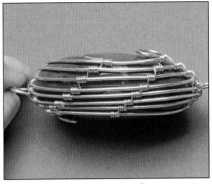

6 Place the stone in the partial frame and form the frame around the stone. Shape ovals of decreasing size in the 18-gauge wire on top of the stone while holding the stone in the frame.

7 Each time you add an oval to the frame, bind with the 24-gauge wire. It is easiest to add one oval section to the frame at a time.

8 Add 3–4 ovals to the frame. Trim the wire end to approximately 1–1½ in. (26–38mm) and shape a small spiral on top of the stone.

9 Finish the necklace by connecting 20-gauge beaded wrapped loops. Connect the hook to one side and the extender chain to the other with wrapped loops. String a gemstone bead and spacers on the head pin and connect it to the end of the extender chain with a wrapped loop.

Beach stones I gathered in Cape Cod were the inspiration for this project. Even if your stone has a drilled hole, you can adapt this technique to fit.

About the author

Irina Miech has been involved in the beading and jewelry world since 1989, when she was traveling in Morocco and a marketplace vendor showed her how to make her first wire loop. She fell in love with the beautiful jewelry and the beads she found overseas and knew there was nothing like them available in the United States at that time. She started a small import business, supplying stores and galleries throughout the U.S. The import business became a boutique called Eclectica, which has evolved into the 6,000-square-foot retail operation and classroom studio she oversees today in Brookfield, Wisconsin. There she sells everything a beader needs to create beautiful jewelry—beads, gemstones, pearls, wire, findings, tools, metal clay, and more. Her Bead Studio offers instruction in wirework, stringing and stitching projects, and metal clay.

Irina is the author of three how-to books on metal clay jewelry, *Metal Clay for Beaders*, published in 2006, *More Metal Clay for Beaders* (2007), and *Inventive Metal Clay for Beaders* (2008), all published by Kalmbach Books. Irina has a bachelor's degree from the University of Wisconsin–Milwaukee, where she studied international relations and the Russian language. She lives with her husband and sons in southeastern Wisconsin.

Acknowledgments

I would like to thank my husband, Tony Miech, for his unwavering support of my work; Lauren Walsh for her writing advice; and my sons, Zachary and David, for their inspirational encouragement and love. I would like to thank my editor, Mary Wohlgemuth, and the rest of the Kalmbach staff for their invaluable assistance. I would also like to thank my wonderful store staff for all of their enthusiastic help and continual support.

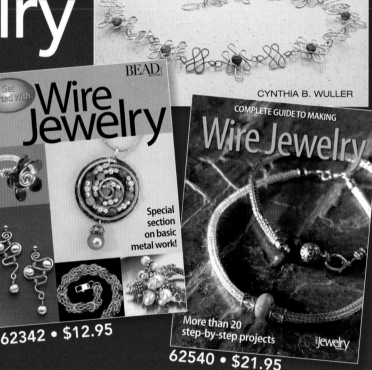